THE JOY OF SKETCHING

First published in Great Britain in 2017 by Little Acorns Publishing.

ISBN: 978-0-9568080-3-5

www.vicbearcroft.co.uk

Little Acorns Publishing
78 Grove Street
Balderton
Newark
Nottinghamshire
NG24 3AS
(44) 1636 651699

This book is dedicated to Liz, for all her patience and hard work in putting this book together; creating order from my rambling thoughts.

INTRODUCTION

I am an artist by profession, which means that I get to spend my time drawing and painting for exhibitions, writing articles for magazines, creating tutorial books and DVDs, and travelling around the country teaching at workshops and demonstrations.

My job is, without question, a full-time commitment, so when I get time, I like to relax. By far my favourite way of relaxing is on the sofa of an evening, with a sketchbook and pencil, doodling or sketching. Most of the time this takes the form of visualising ideas that find their way into my head from various sources.

Undoubtedly, my main source of inspiration is a small lake and wooded area close to my home, which I call Bunny Wood. This is where I regularly walk my dogs. Despite being a relatively small area, there are so many things to see. Here I can observe the continually changing face of nature throughout the year; wildflowers come and go, along with mushrooms and toadstools of all varieties. There is wildlife in abundance: rabbits, squirrels, birds, waterfowl, frogs, toads, butterflies and moths. All manner of creatures make themselves known when you take the time to look.

If I see an interesting tree stump, roots or bark texture, perhaps a cluster of fungi, I begin to imagine what other unseen woodland creatures might there be, hiding away from prying human eyes. In my mind I have visions of fairies, trolls and trees with faces, all of which begin to tell me their stories.

These 'stories' are temporarily put aside while I get on with my usual work and then resurface in the evening as I relax on the sofa with my sketchbook.

One of my other forms of relaxation is reading. I have a particular fondness for supernatural and fairy stories. I love to rescue old classic children's books from charity shops and often re-read the stories I loved as a child, visualising the characters and, of course, re-imagining these characters in my sketchbooks.

Sometimes the inspiration for my 'sofa sketches' comes from listening to music, as certain melodies and some song lyrics can also suggest images for sketching.

Finally, I must acknowledge the influence that our own animals; dogs, cats and wild rescues have on my sketches, their individual personalities and actions are a great source of inspiration for me, and occasionally they have been known to star in their own versions of my favourite movies!

Some of my 'sofa sketches' may find their way to becoming more complete illustrations, perhaps in ink and colour, but mostly I like to keep them as they are, fresh, relatively quick artworks in their own right; something to look back on as a memory of a certain time and place.

Now I'm sharing these memories and inspirations with you, and hopefully they will inspire you to take up 'sofa sketching' yourself.

Stories, Films and Music

PETER PAN

I happened to be away for a few days at an exhibition. In the room where I was staying was a bookcase with assorted reading material. As luck would have it, there was a copy of one of my childhood favourites, 'Peter Pan and Wendy'. This was just the bedtime relaxation therapy I needed after a long day demonstrating at the exhibition.

It wasn't long before I realised how different an experience it was, re-reading this wonderful story of 'a place between sleep and awake, where we can still remember dreaming', after many years. The narrative itself seemed to be more 'grown-up', and so the images I formed in my head of the characters were different from those I remembered as a child.

After the exhibition, when I got home, these characters were still in my mind so, of course, I had to visualise some of them in a series of sketches to clear the way for other things.

Here is my re-imagining of Peter Pan. I made him slightly darker than the character I remember as a much smaller child than I am now; a Peter for the modern era and perhaps a touch more androgynous, as I believe he should represent all those (boys *and* girls) who never want to grow up.

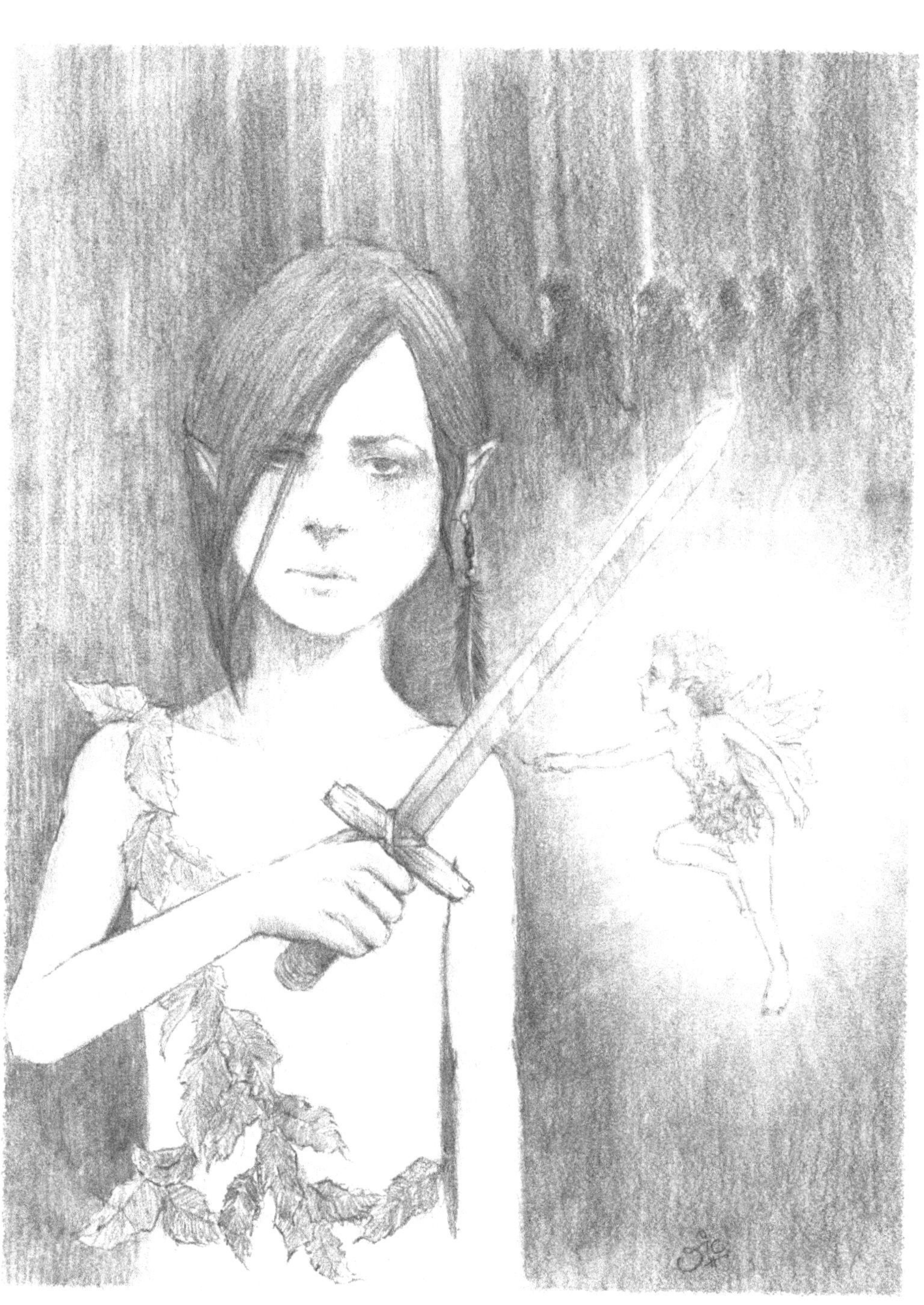

'Never Grow Up'

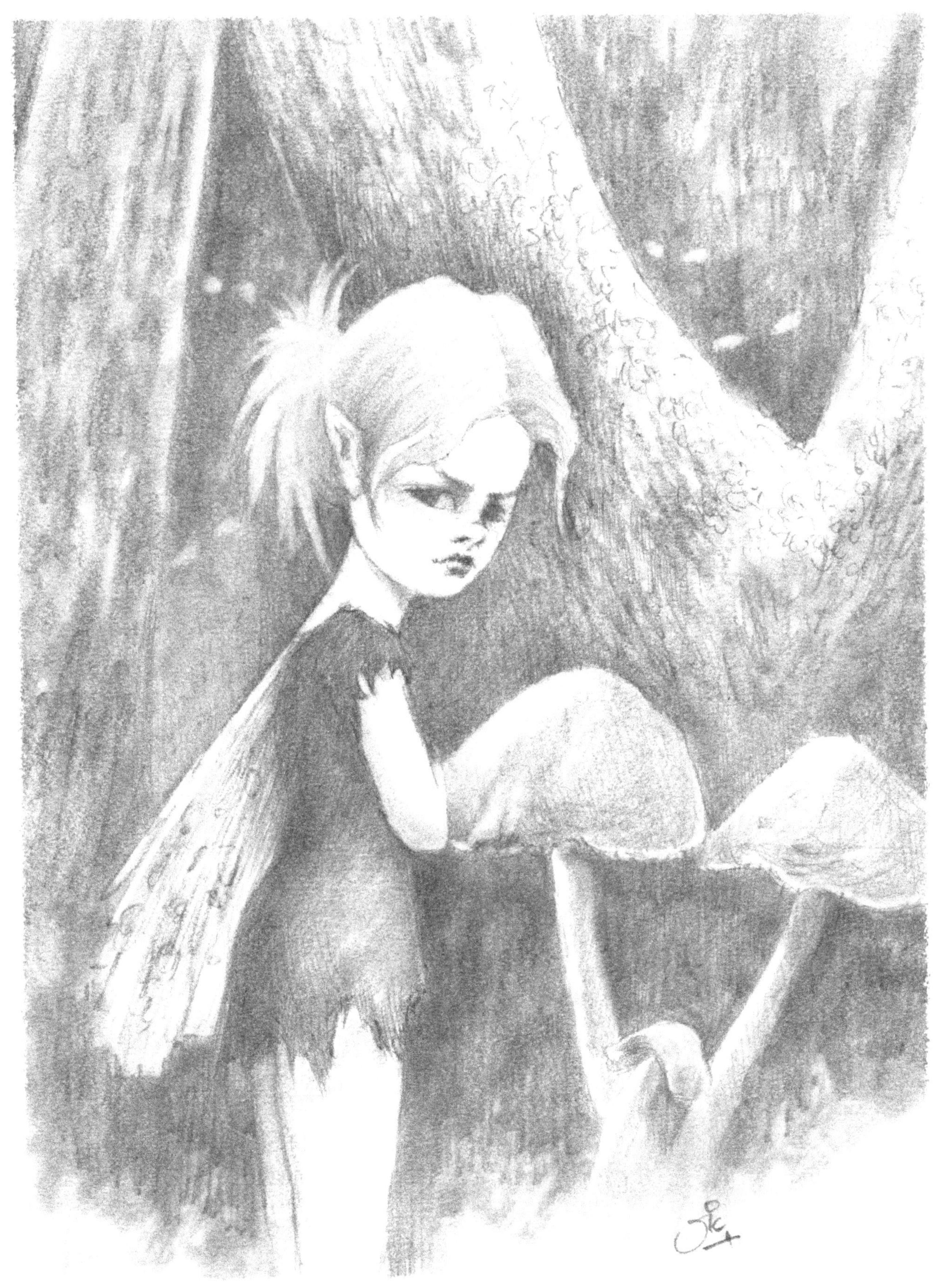

'The Green-Eyed Monster'

Tinker Bell was a feisty little madam. Jealous of other girls getting close to Peter (i.e., Wendy and Tiger Lily), she would often fly, quite literally, into a jealous rage, uttering her favourite phrase, 'You silly ass!'

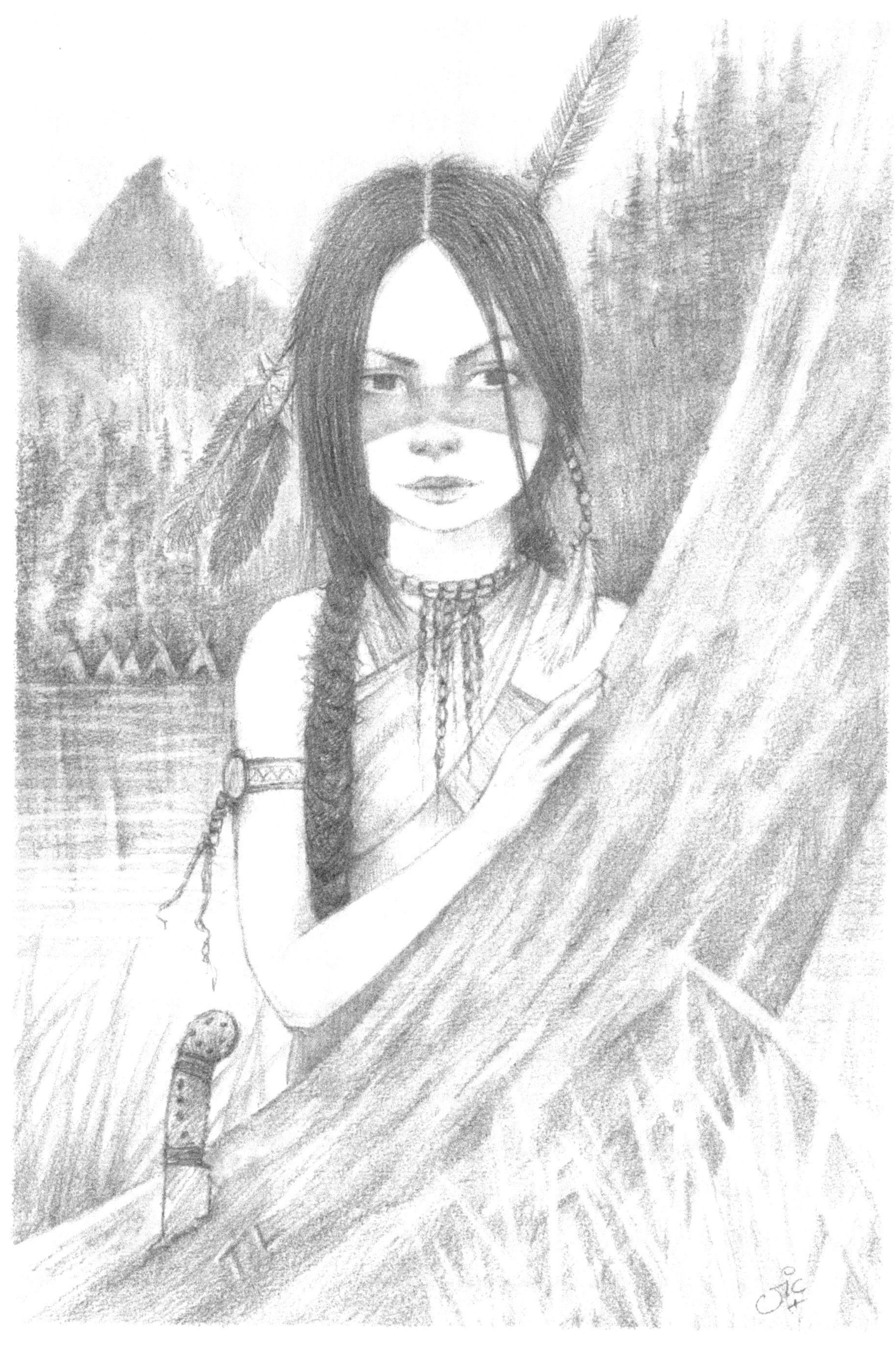

'The Warrior Princess'

Although Tiger Lily doesn't have a lot of involvement in the story, she nevertheless comes across as a strong, determined warrior, and this is how I imagined her in that role.

ALICE'S ADVENTURES IN WONDERLAND

A perennial favourite since its first publication in 1865, 'Alice's Adventures in Wonderland' has never lost its story-telling power to stimulate the imagination.

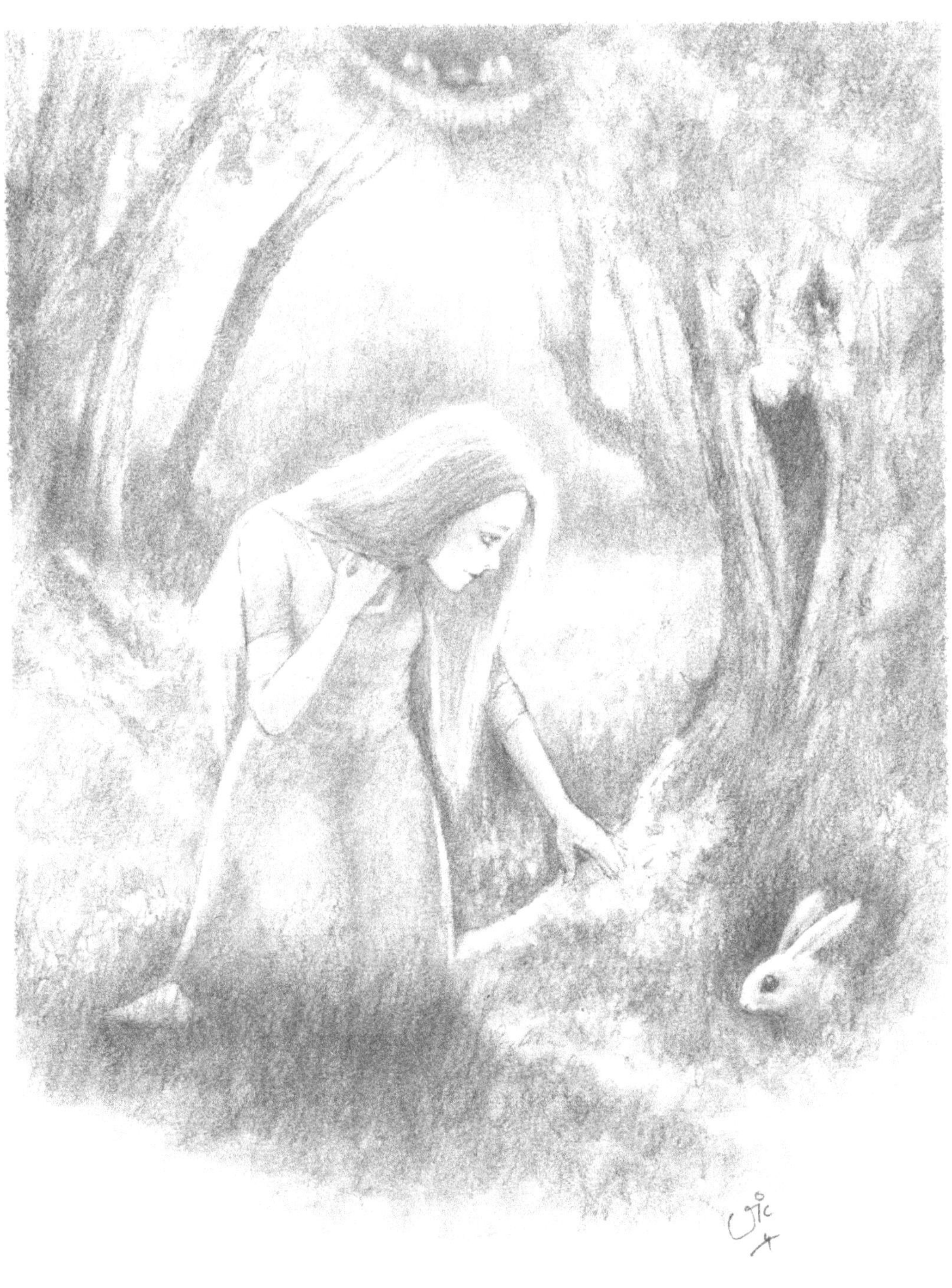

'Alice'

While walking my dogs in Bunny Wood, I came across a tree with a rather surprised expression; and so began the inspiration for an evening's sofa sketch. Beginning with the tree, the rest of the sketch grew around it, probably influenced by my flicking through my old books the day before, including a 1933 copy of 'Alice in Wonderland', and, naturally, Bunny Wood itself, attempting to capture the early morning light of our local enchanted spot.

Here is another version of Alice that I had in mind. As I daydreamed about Bunny Wood and the stories still to be discovered, I wondered whether Alice, on her return from Wonderland, dreamed of the adventures she had there. This sketch is inspired by a particular section of the poem by Lewis Carroll that prefaces the story.

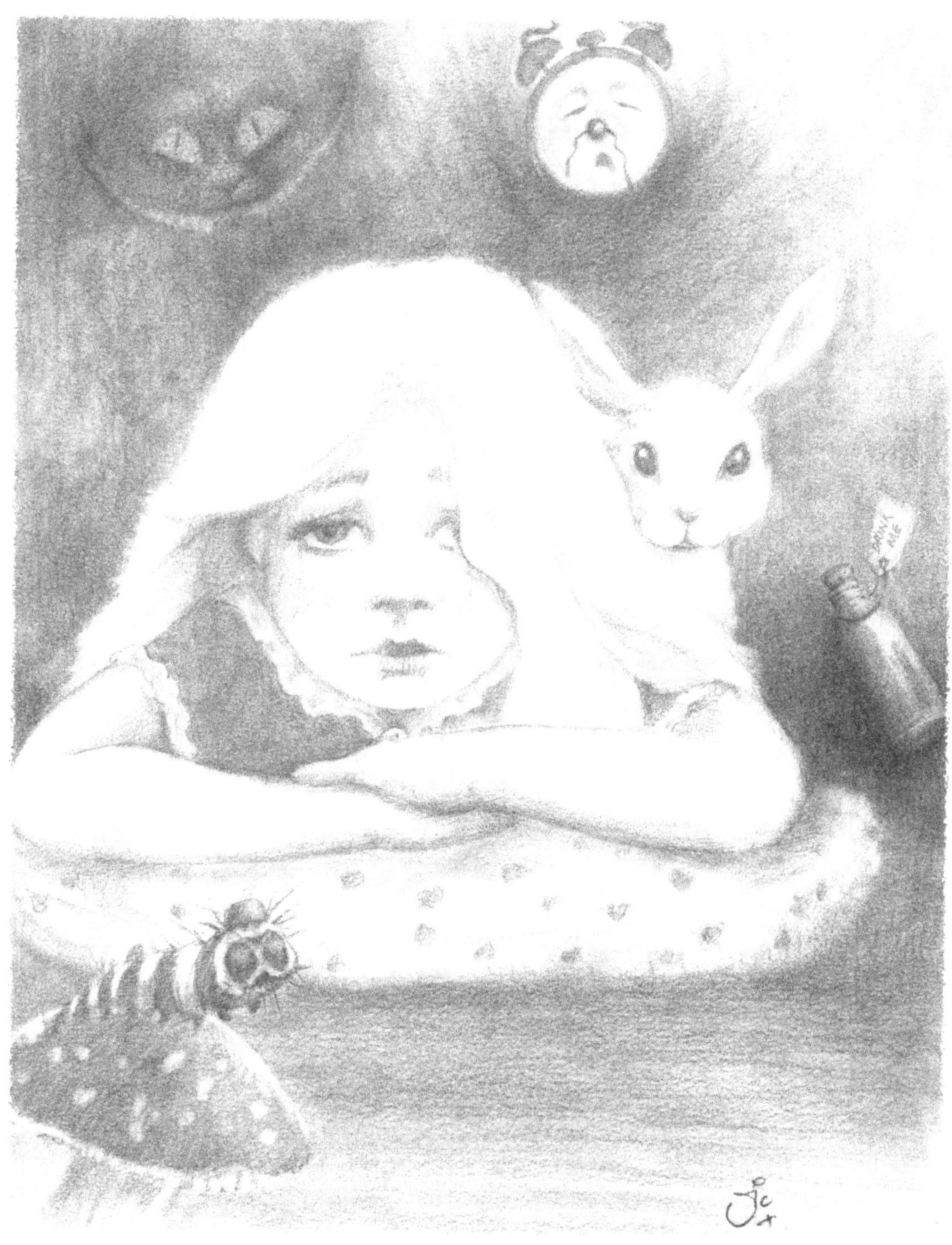

'Dreams of Wonderland'

'Anon, to sudden silence won,
In fancy they pursue
The dream-child moving through a land
Of wonders wild and new...'

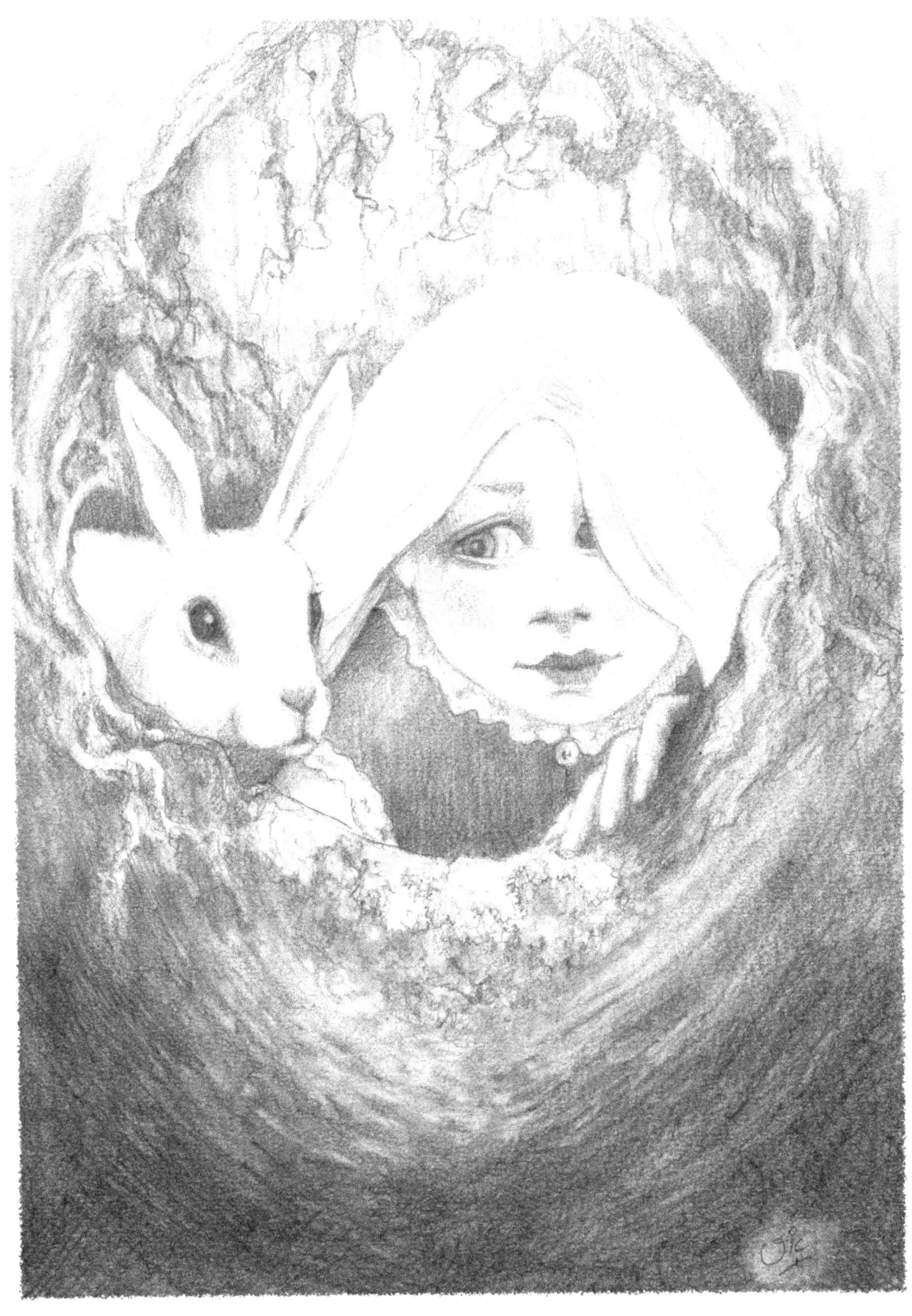

'Down the Rabbit Hole'

This sketch is a follow up to 'Dreams of Wonderland'. Often the beginning of an adventure, a story, or even an illustration is the most exciting part; a leap into the unknown. There is still so much to wonder at, if you believe.

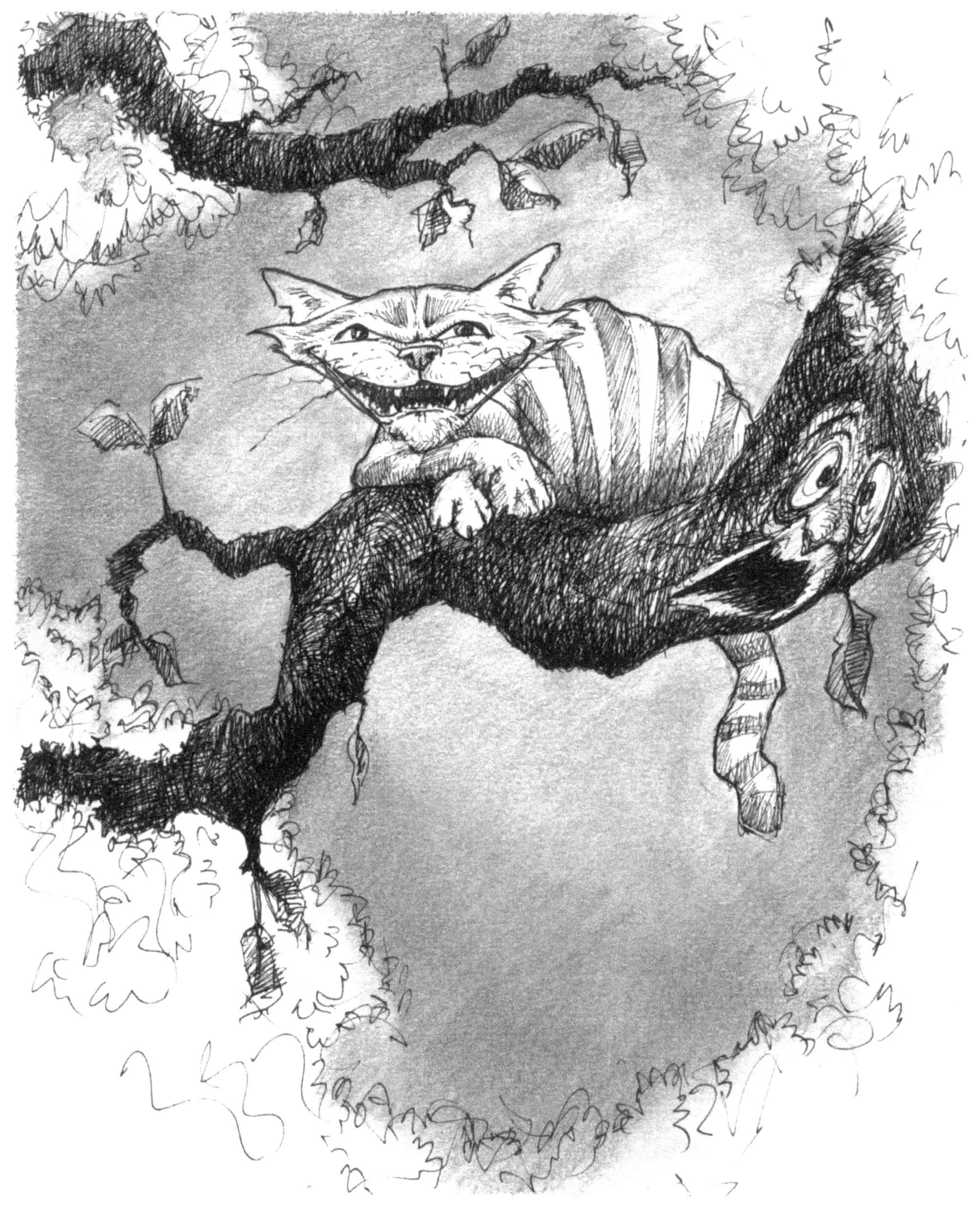

'We're All Mad Here'

This pen and graphite sketch was actually my first 'Alice in Wonderland' sketch, inspired by one of the great fairy tale illustrators, Arthur Rackham, and his wonderful trees. 'We're All Mad Here' later became a full-colour illustration in my 'Drawing and Painting Cats' book. The Cheshire Cat was loosely based on our ginger cat, Forrest.

THE WONDERFUL WIZARD OF OZ

'The Wizard of Oz' is such an enduring classic tale; both the original Frank Baum story and the 1939 film that I remember being totally captivated by as a child. The writing and movie imagery still have the power to inspire; so much so that when I began working on 'Drawing and Painting Cats', I knew I had to include an illustration of possibly my favourite character, the cowardly lion. I found the perfect subject in 'Tiny', a lion from the Big Cat Sanctuary in Kent, UK.

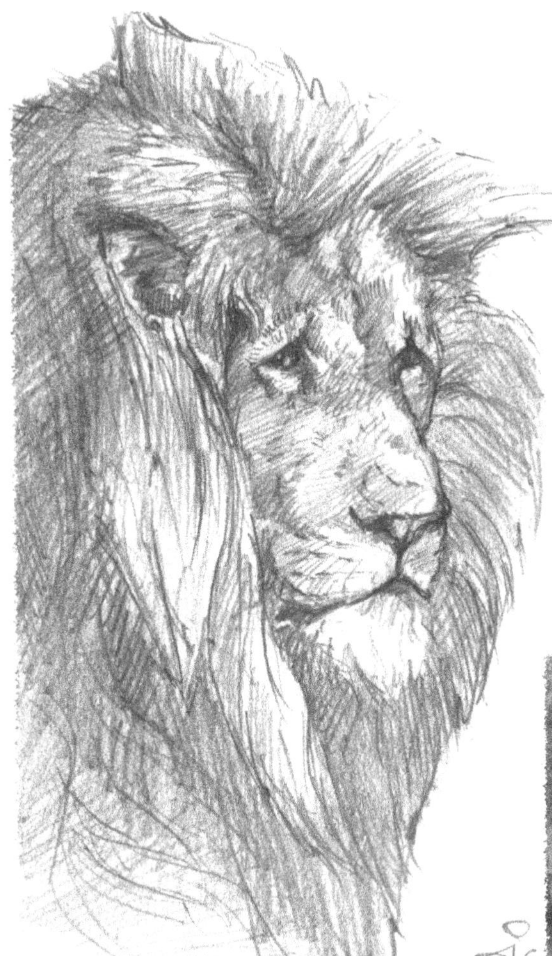

My first sketch was just of Tiny's head, trying to create the right expression of apprehension in the lion's face.

'Tiny'

The second sketch was a visualisation of the whole scene; our 'hero' about to follow the yellow brick road into the dark heart of the haunted forest. These sketches formed the basis of the final ink illustration, 'Oh My!', which naturally included some 'Rackham-esque' trees!

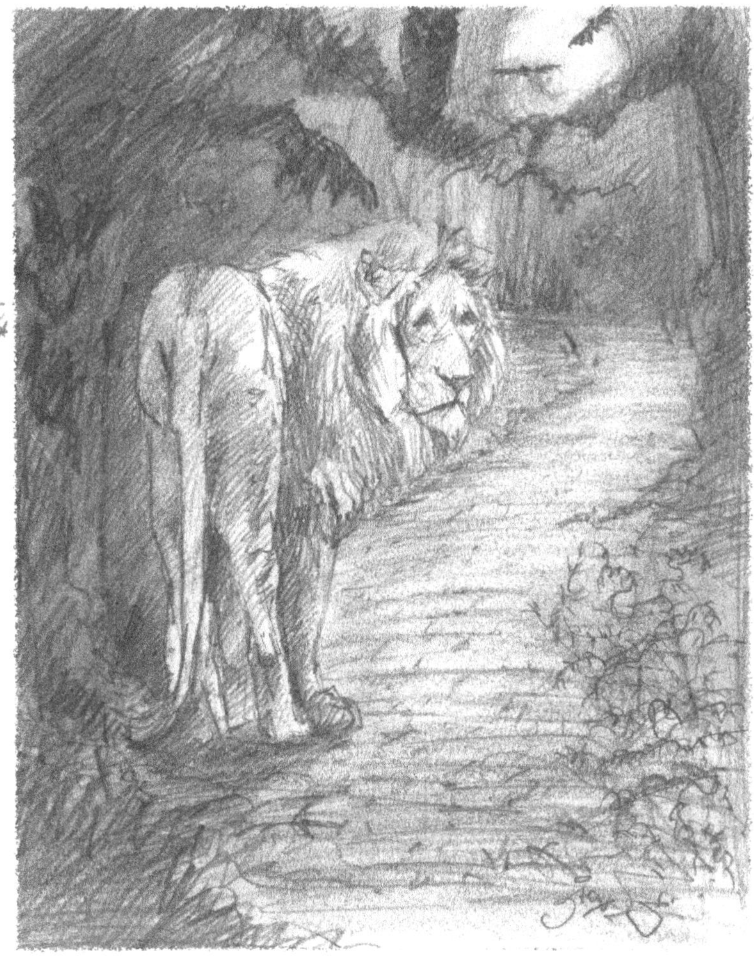

'Oh My!'

RED RIDING HOOD

This has to be one of the most popular children's stories of all time. Red Riding Hood and the wolf have been depicted countless times in books, films and illustrations, and, after watching a recent film version of the tale, I wanted to add my own take on the characters.
I have a particular fondness for wolves, and have been lucky to view them at close quarters in sanctuaries here in the UK and in the USA for many years, seeing them as the intelligent, non-aggressive animals they really are. This, of course, had a real influence on how I depicted the wolf in the following sketches.

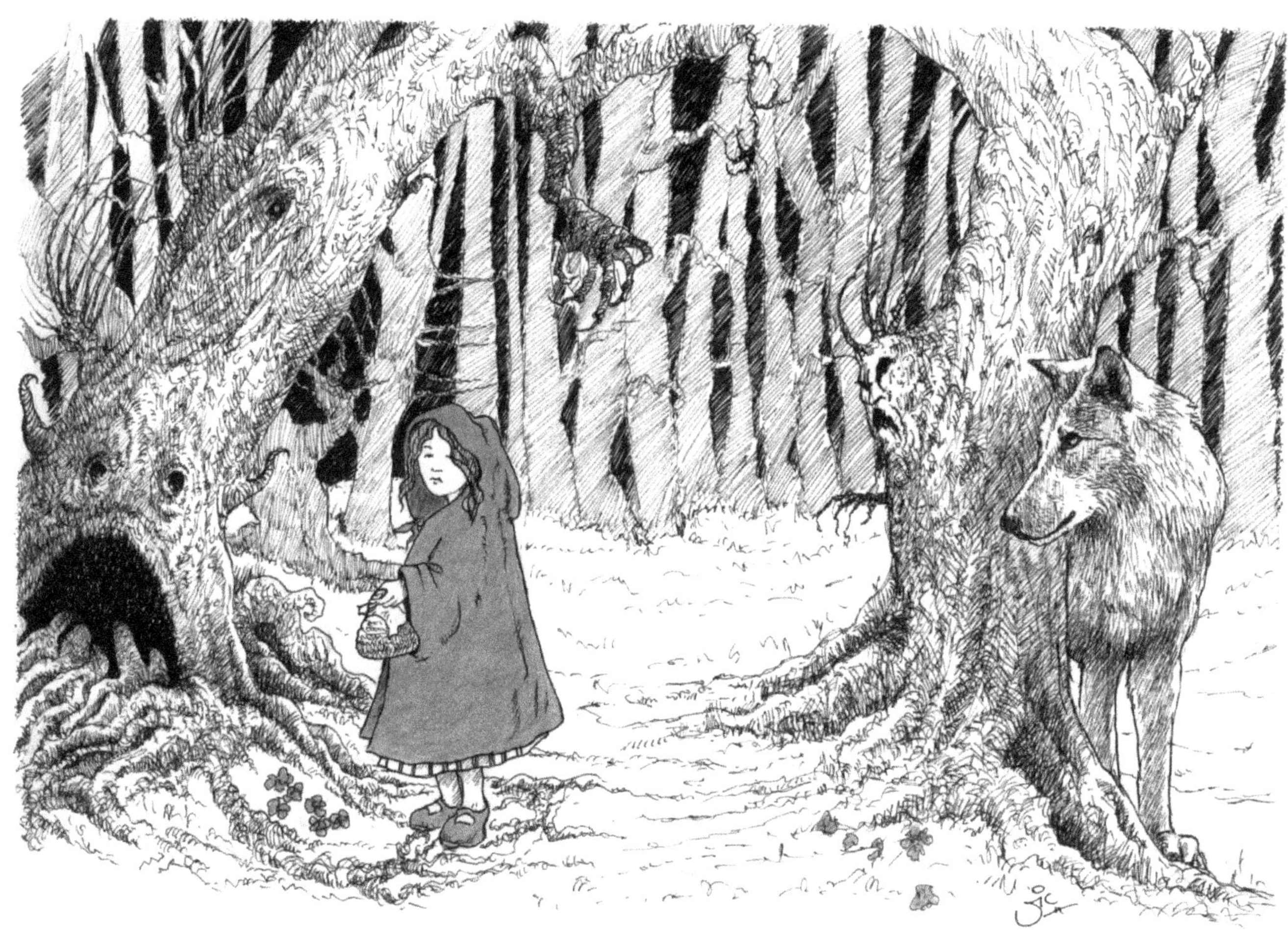

'Red #1'

This is the first sketch I made of the story, with Red Riding Hood as a child; a familiar depiction for many, I'm sure. My particular slant on this representation was to turn the wolf into more of a Guardian Angel, looking to protect her from more malevolent forces in the forest.

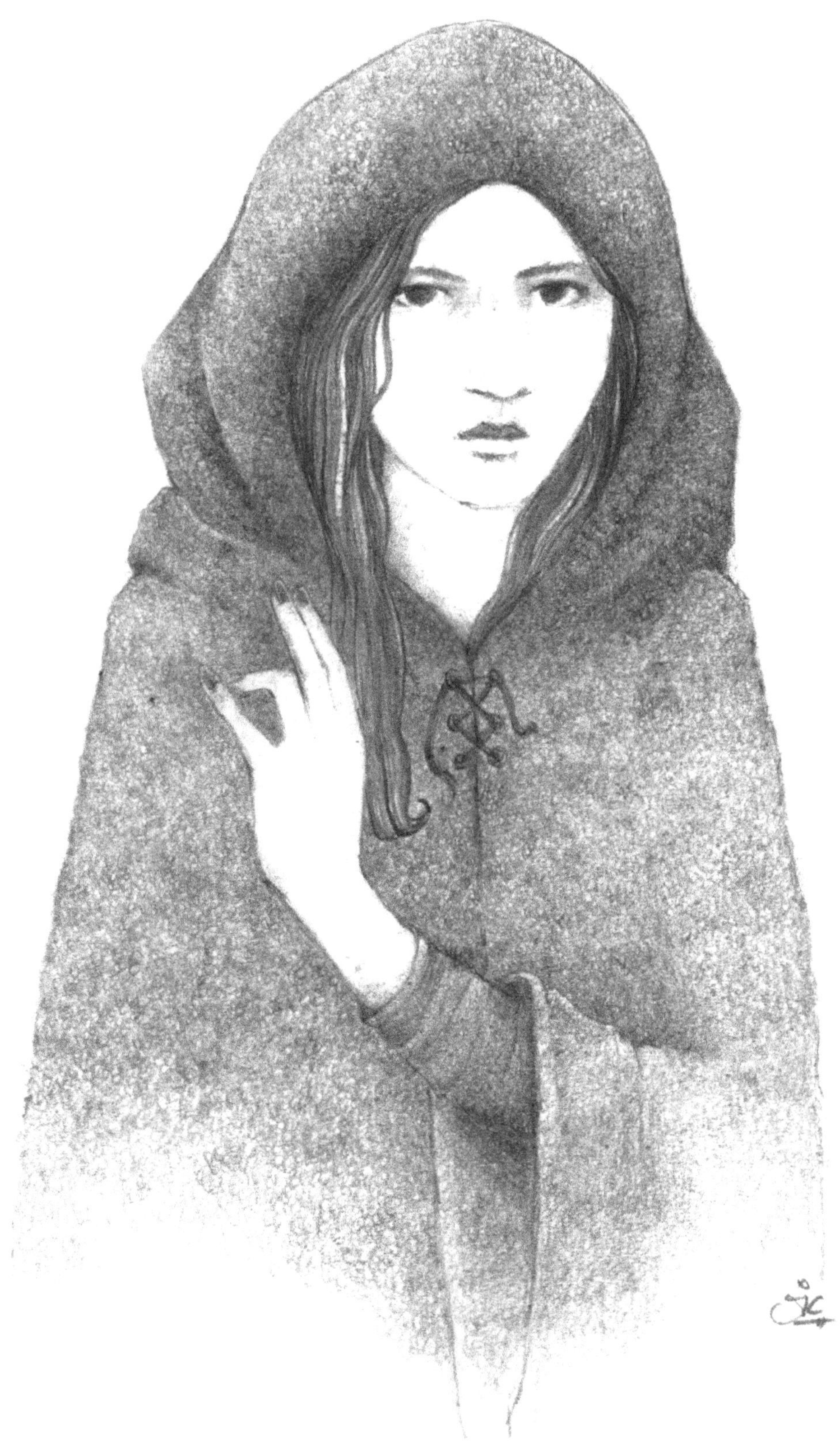

'Red #2'

This sketch began as a character doodle, an attempt to imagine what Red Riding Hood would look like a few years after the 'grandma' incident. A couple of hours later it had turned into an exercise in texturing her cloak, the result of which I was happy with, and I learned something more about creating textures with a pencil. Time spent doodling is always time well spent.

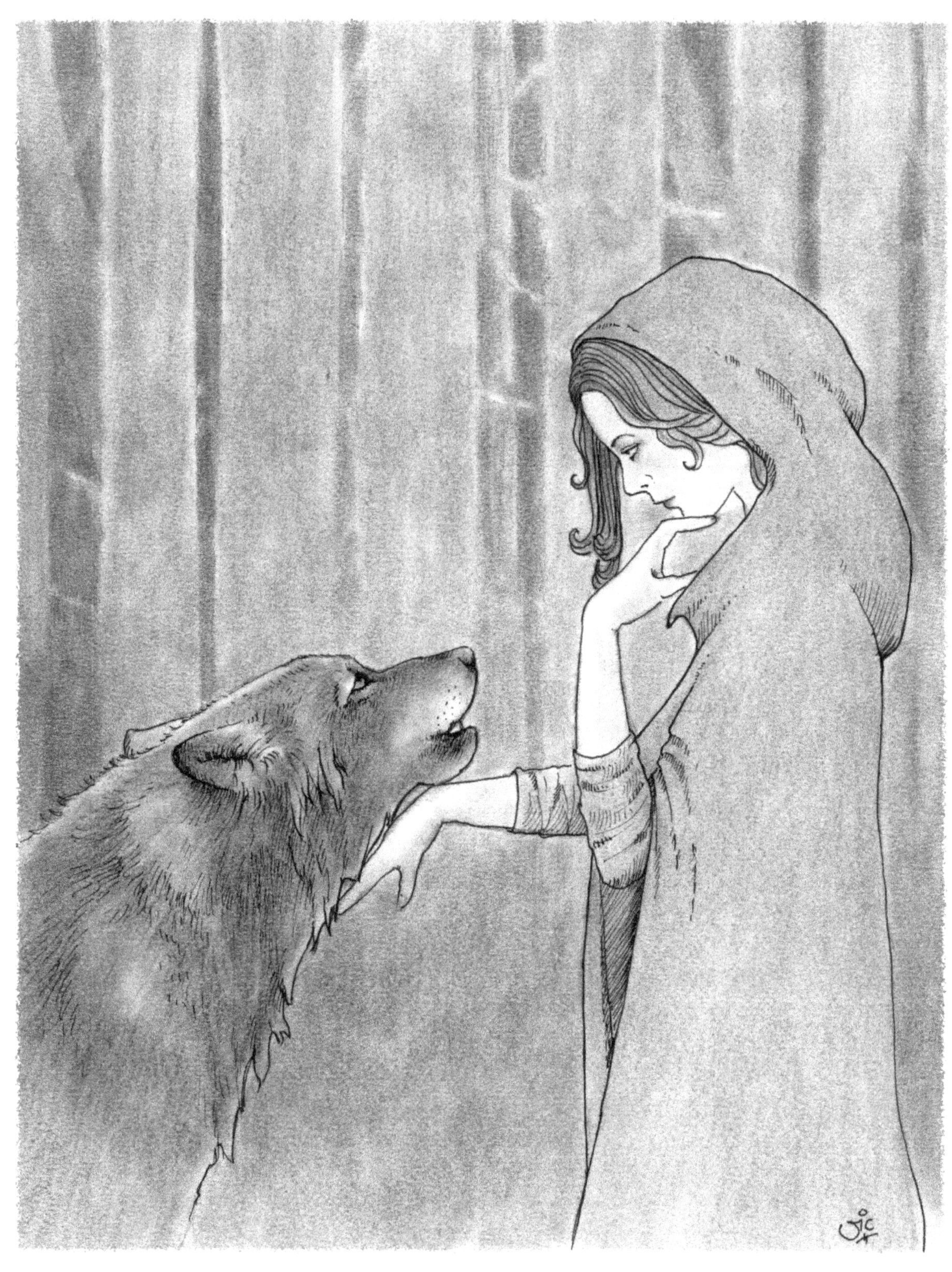

'Red #3'

In this sketch I decided to update 'Red #1', in which our scarlet-cloaked heroine is now a young woman and looking forward to some, as yet untold, exciting adventures in the forest with her childhood guardian and now lupine soul mate. I really wanted to capture the close relationship between Red Riding Hood and the older wolf.

GOLDILOCKS

While I was spending a few days away at an exhibition, the subject of porridge came up at breakfast time, appropriately enough I suppose. However, for the rest of the day, images of Goldilocks and the three bears kept popping into my head. So, that evening in my room, I started this sketch, finishing it the following day in between demonstrating my more 'serious' artwork techniques at the exhibition. I had a lot of fun imagining what was going on in the characters' minds, and trying to create appropriate expressions for all four of them.

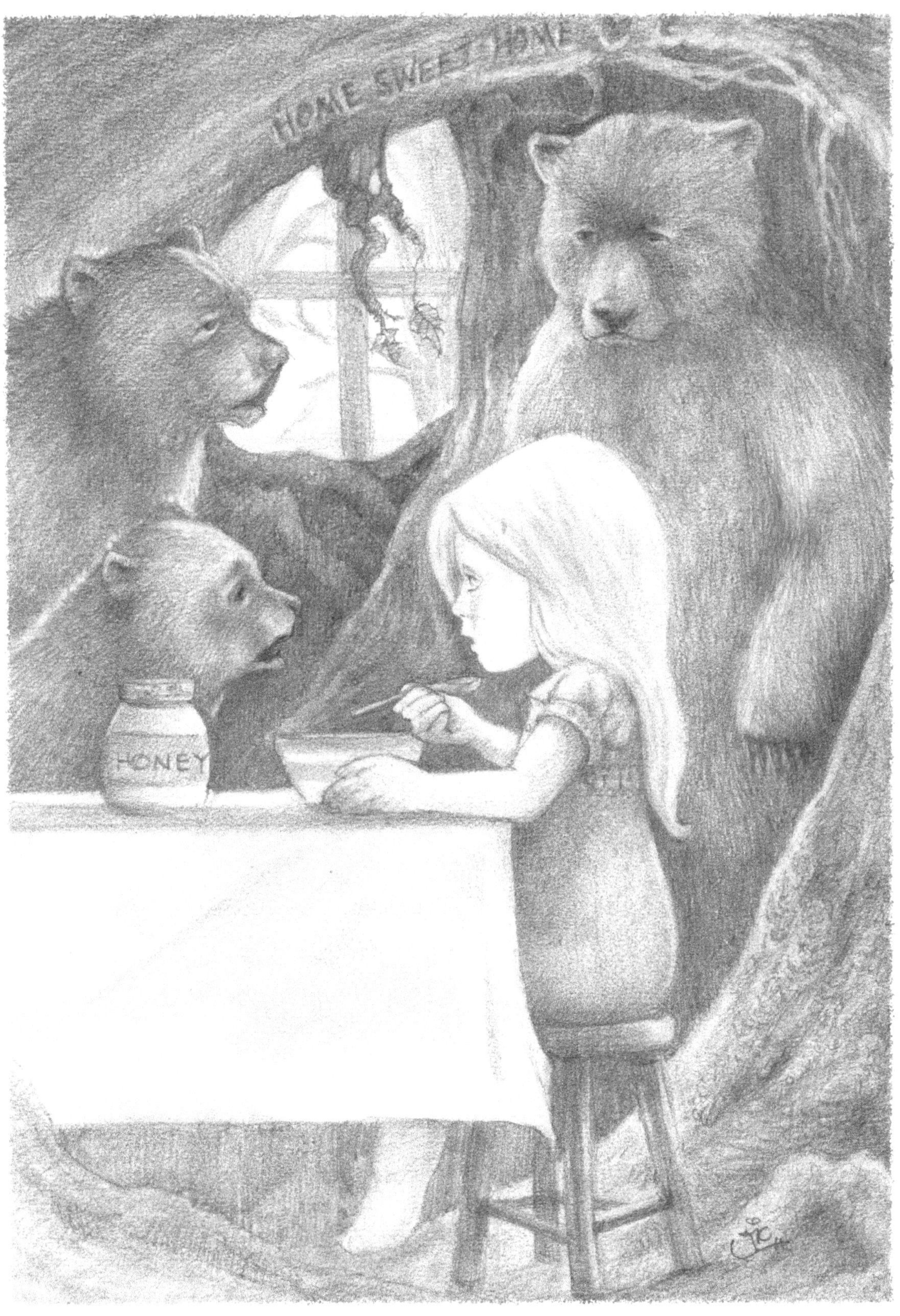

'Goldilocks'

LITTLE MISS MUFFET

This turned into a two evening 'sofa sketch'. It could have easily been sketched in a couple of hours, except I decided to give Miss 'M' dark curly hair instead of the traditional blonde locks, for more 'attitude', so that bit took ages. I also had to use a 'selfie' reference of my own hand to show her holding the spoon, because I couldn't seem to get that bit right.

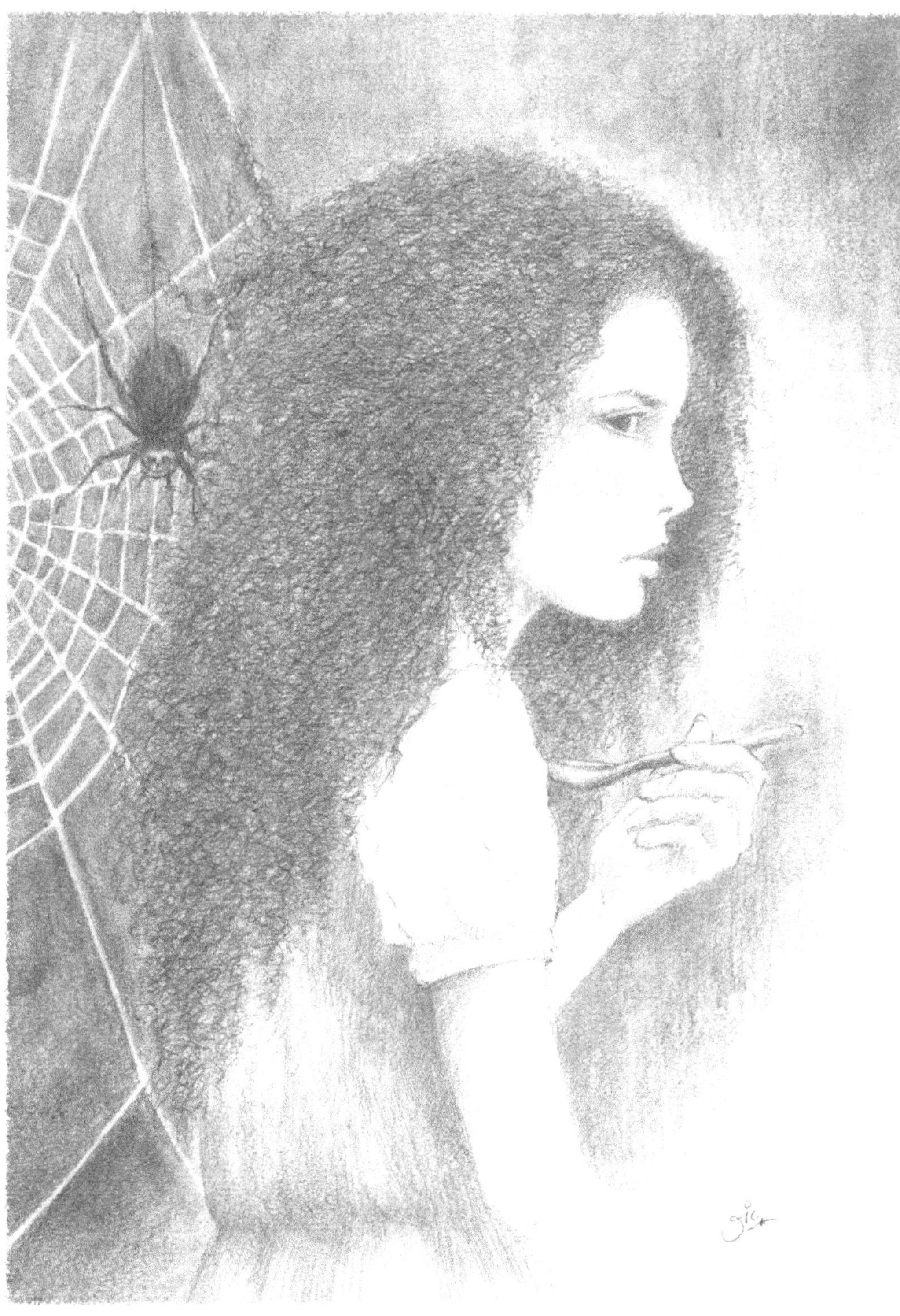

'Along Came a Spider'

'Little Miss Muffet sat on her tuffet, eating her curds and whey.

Along came a spider and sat down beside her, but she wasn't scared... no way!'

BEAUTY AND THE BEAST

Inspired by the original story of 'Beauty and the Beast', this was technically a two-part sketch, as I had already drawn Beast, based on one of the lions at the big cat sanctuary in Kent, UK. Some weeks later I added Beauty and the rose which was plucked from the Beast's garden by Beauty's father, the singular action which caused all the fuss that followed.

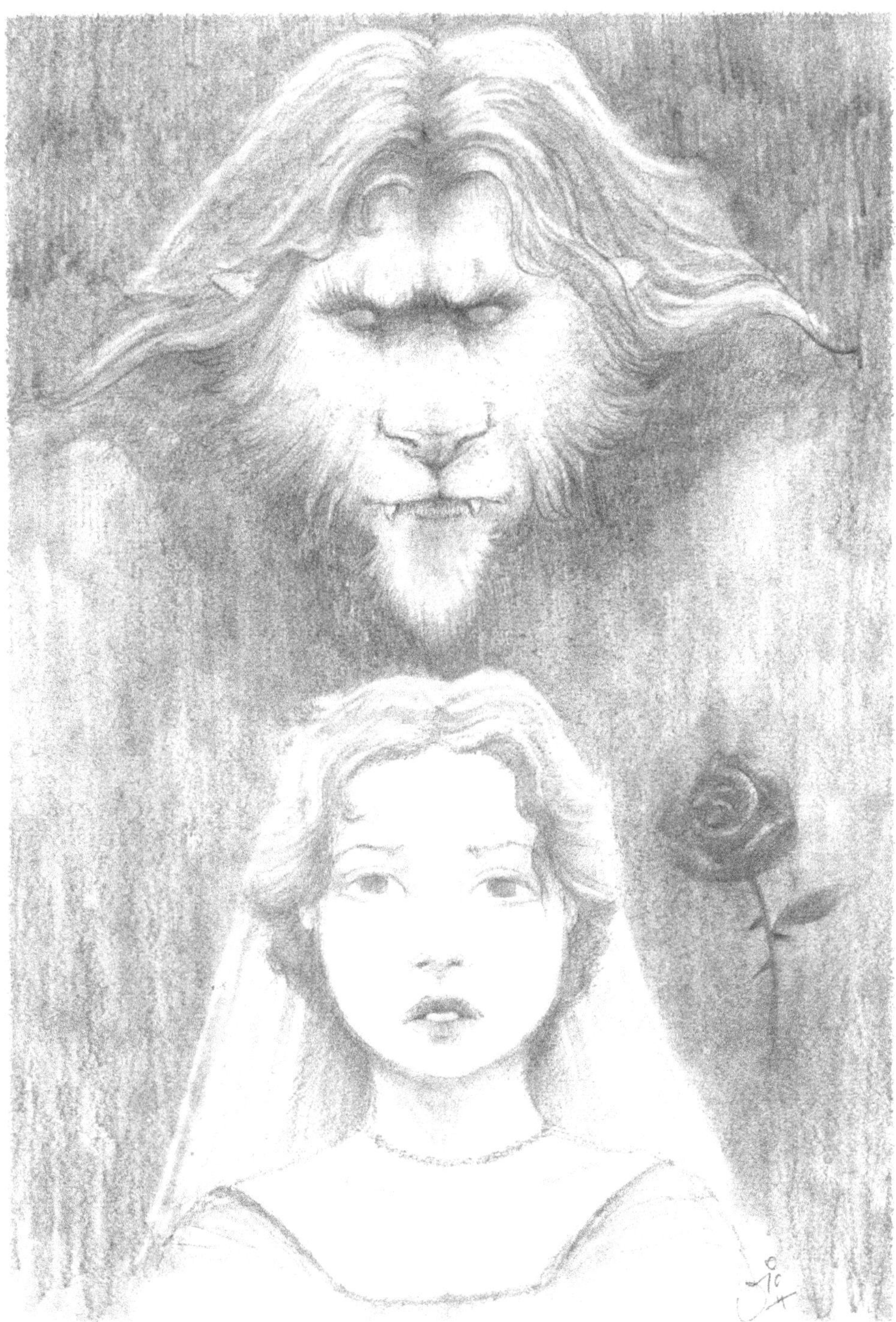

'Beauty and the Beast'

'Welcome Beauty, banish fear,
You are queen and mistress here.
Speak your wishes, speak your will,
Swift obedience meets them still.'

(Gabrielle-Suzanne Barbot deVilleneuve, 1740)

RAPUNZEL

Occasionally I get carried away with the ideas that come to mind during the sketching process; that is one of the reasons why I enjoy this art form so much.

As doodles can turn into sketches, so sketches can turn into illustrations, and this is what started to happen with 'Rapunzel'.

I had often imagined Rapunzel as one of those tragic Pre-Raphaelite characters, with long red hair instead of the golden tresses she was better-known for. Even the idea that she was imprisoned in a tower suggests overtones of 'The Lady of Shallot' to me.

So here is my almost completed Pre-Raphaelite Rapunzel, locked away in her tower prison. I added the thorn branches to represent barbed wire blocking her escape, even if her hair grew long enough for her to use it as a rope.

Even though the illustration is unfinished, I feel that all the elements are in place for me to either finish it at some point, or re-draw it with ink and colour.

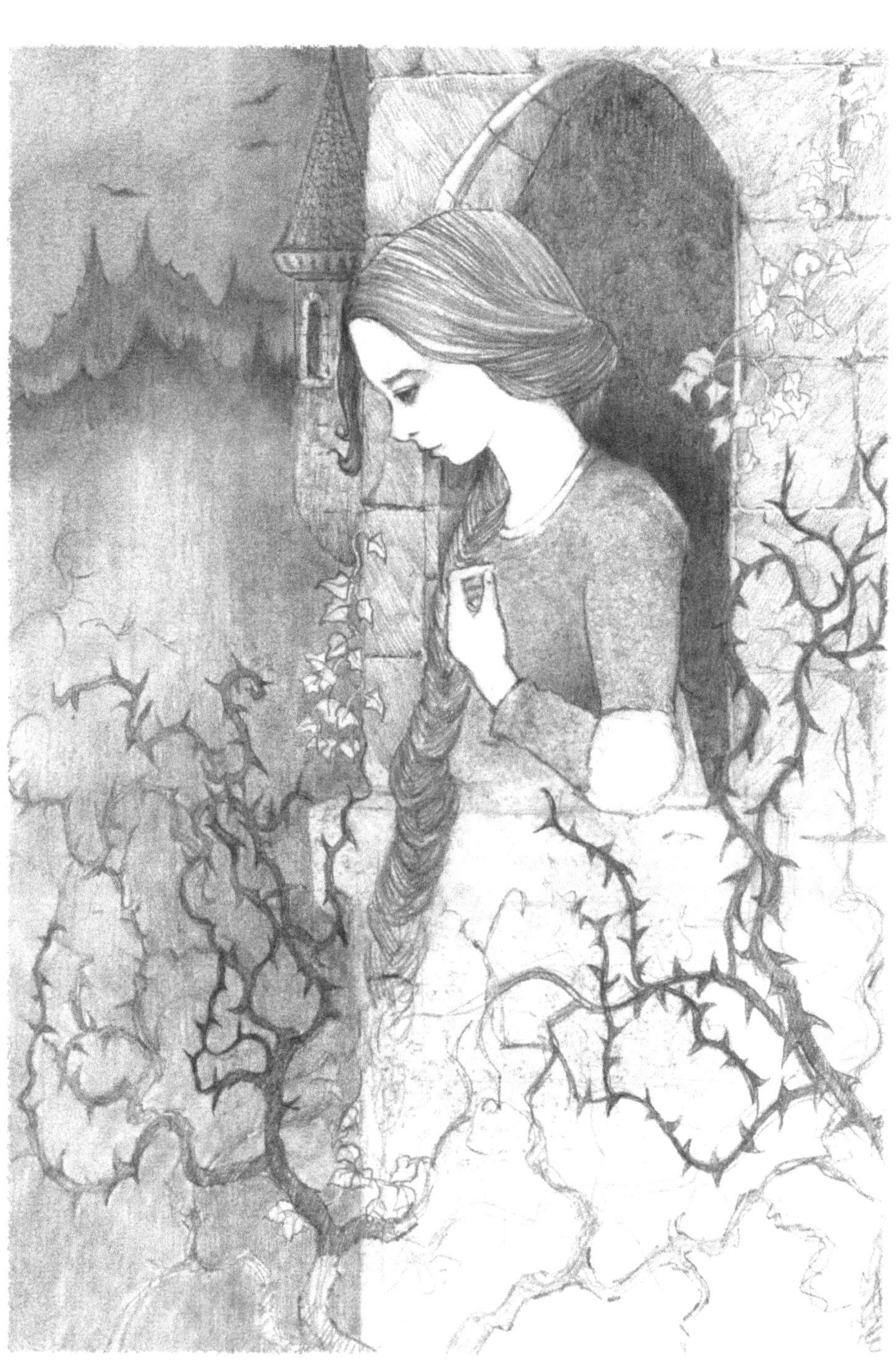

'Rapunzel'

SNOW WHITE

'It is when we are most lost that we sometimes find our truest friends'

'Snow White' is a Grimm brothers classic, with all the elements essential for a good fairy tale; poisoned apple, magic mirror, evil stepmother and so on, and there never has been a shortage of visual interpretations of the story.

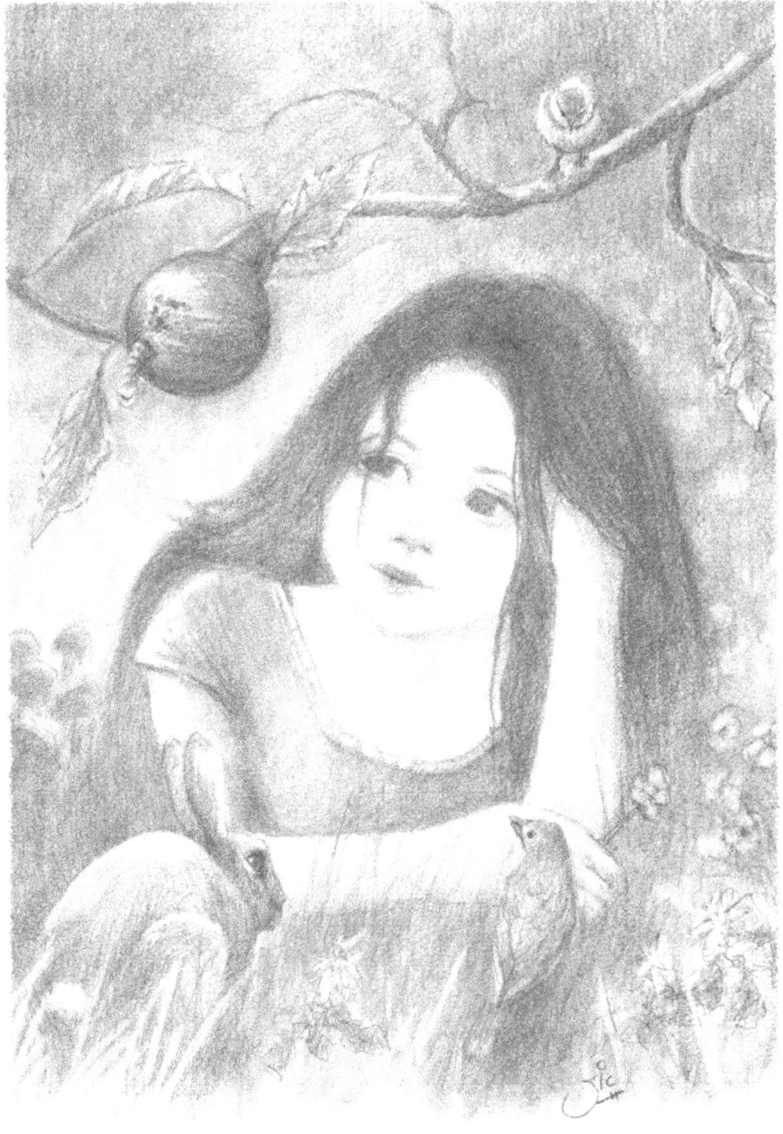

For my own first sketch of Snow White, I decided to focus on the child; happy and carefree in nature's garden. There is, however, a hint of darker times ahead in the apple that she is pondering upon eating.

'Snow White'

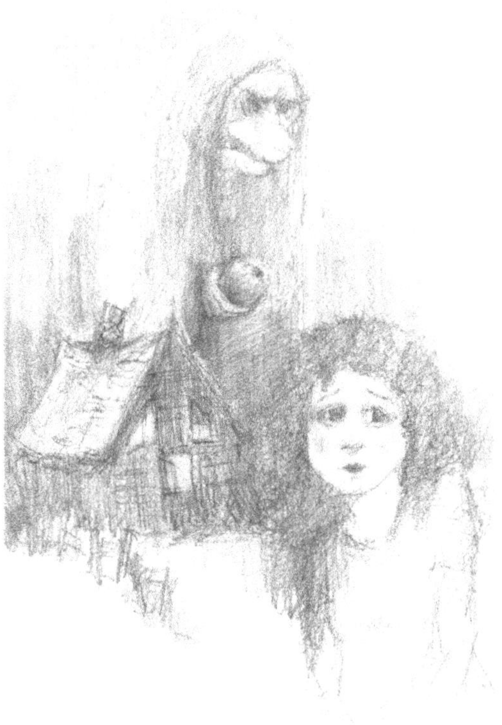

Imagining further into the story, I also did a quick character sketch, featuring a slightly older Snow White, the evil stepmother as the witch, and the home of the seven dwarves.

'Snow White #2'

THE LOST WORLD

The original version of 'The Lost World' by Sir Arthur Conan Doyle is perhaps the story that I have read, listened to and watched so many more times over the years than any other.
'The Lost World' is adventure, science, exploration, good guys, bad guys, ape-men, danger and, of course, dinosaurs; so many ingredients that I love.

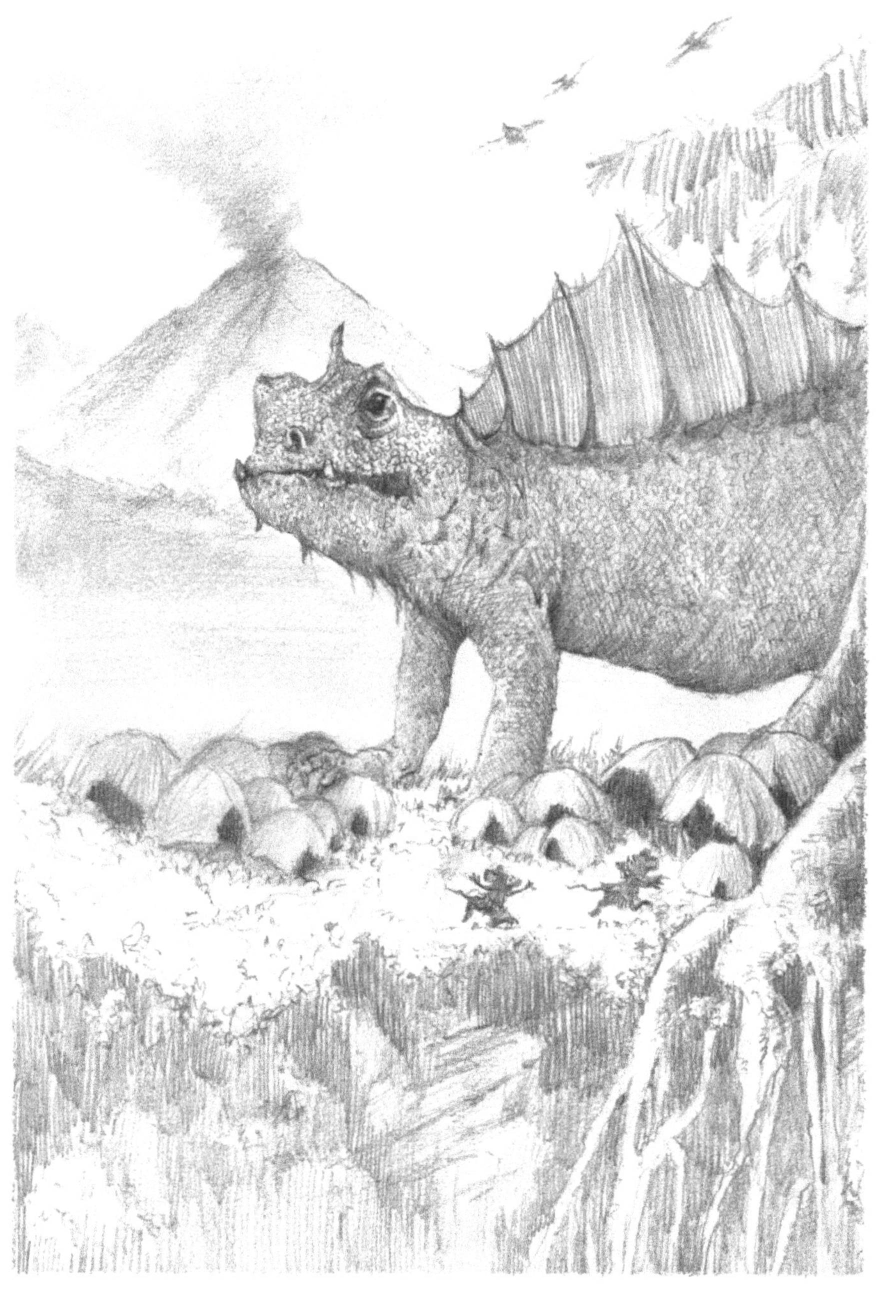

'The Lost World # 1'

One weekend I discovered an abandoned mushroom village while I was walking Elliott, our husky. I began to wonder what might have happened to the inhabitants of such small dwellings; it seemed as if something terrible had scared them away. So one evening in a hotel, prior to a workshop the next day, I thought I'd try to fill in the gaps in the story with a pencil sketch. The 'dinosaur' is based on a lizard from Marwell zoo by the way, with just a touch of 1950's B-Movie make-up added.

Here is another take on 'The Lost World', which owes itself to the Spielberg films as much as Conan Doyle's book. Another visit to Marwell Zoo happened to coincide with an animatronic dinosaur exhibit, the most popular, and my favourite, being the life-size Tyrannosaurus Rex model.
Coincidentally, that same evening in my hotel room, 'Jurassic Park' was showing on the TV. I needed no further excuse to get out my sketchbook and pen than that, of course.
By the time the film had finished, and having raided it for ideas of foliage, the sketch was complete.

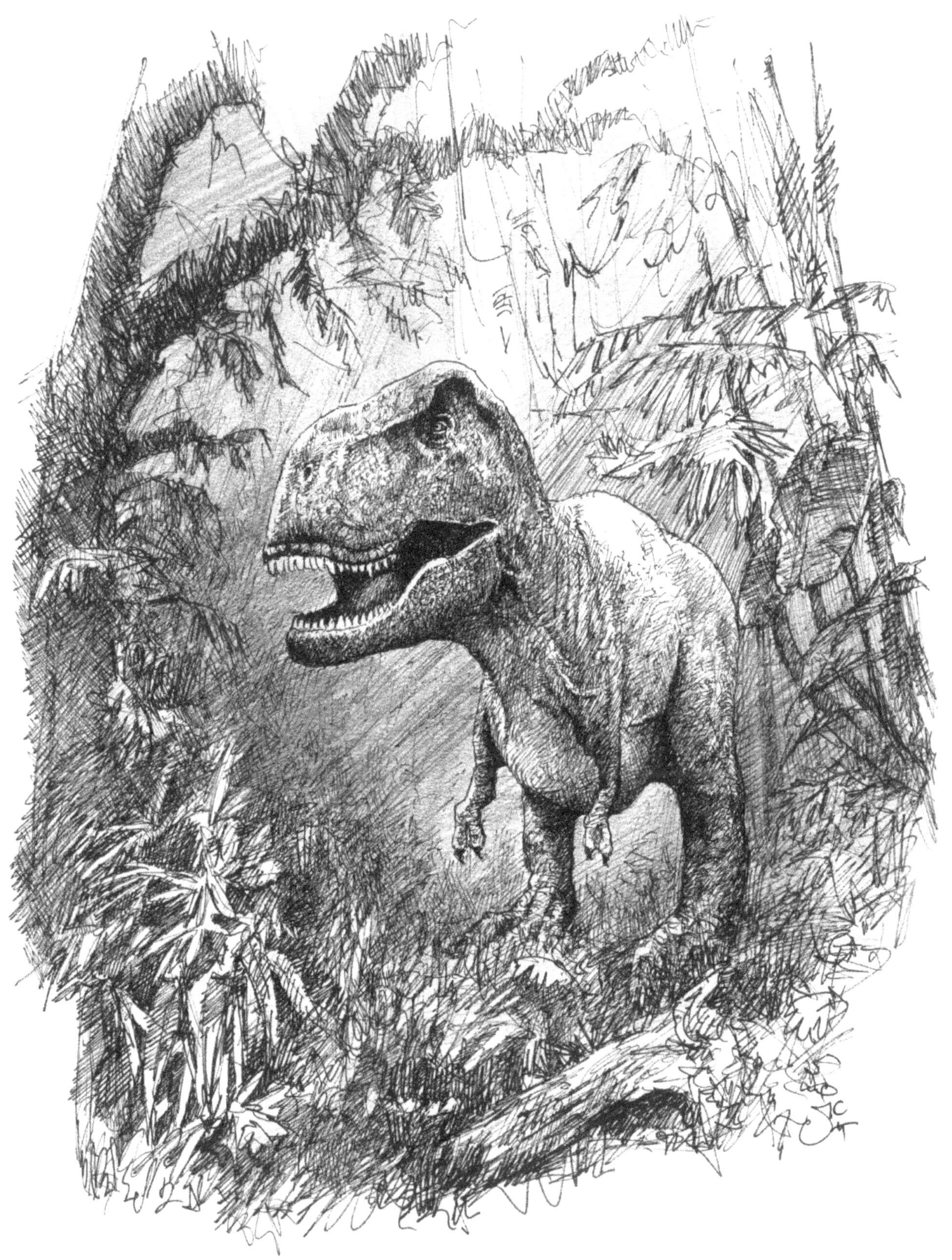

'The Lost World #2'

THE MUSIC BOX

Have you ever thought how the innocent sound of a child's music box seems to take on more sinister connotations after a while? There is a song by one of my favourite bands, Rammstein, called 'Spieluhr', or 'Music Box', the lyrics of which are in German, Rammstein being a German band.
The sound of the song is quite haunting with echoes of a child's music box throughout the melody.
The song is an eerie tale of a child, thought to be dead, being buried with her music box and, one winter's night, coming back to life, accompanied by the haunting melody of the box.
The more I listened to the song, the more images filled my head until one evening I decided to sketch those images.

In this, my second attempt at the sketch, I tried to evoke the eeriness of the story, with the light source beneath the girl highlighting her melancholy. The misty effects were created using a kneadable eraser, while the stopping of her heart in the first part of the story is symbolised in the background tree formation.

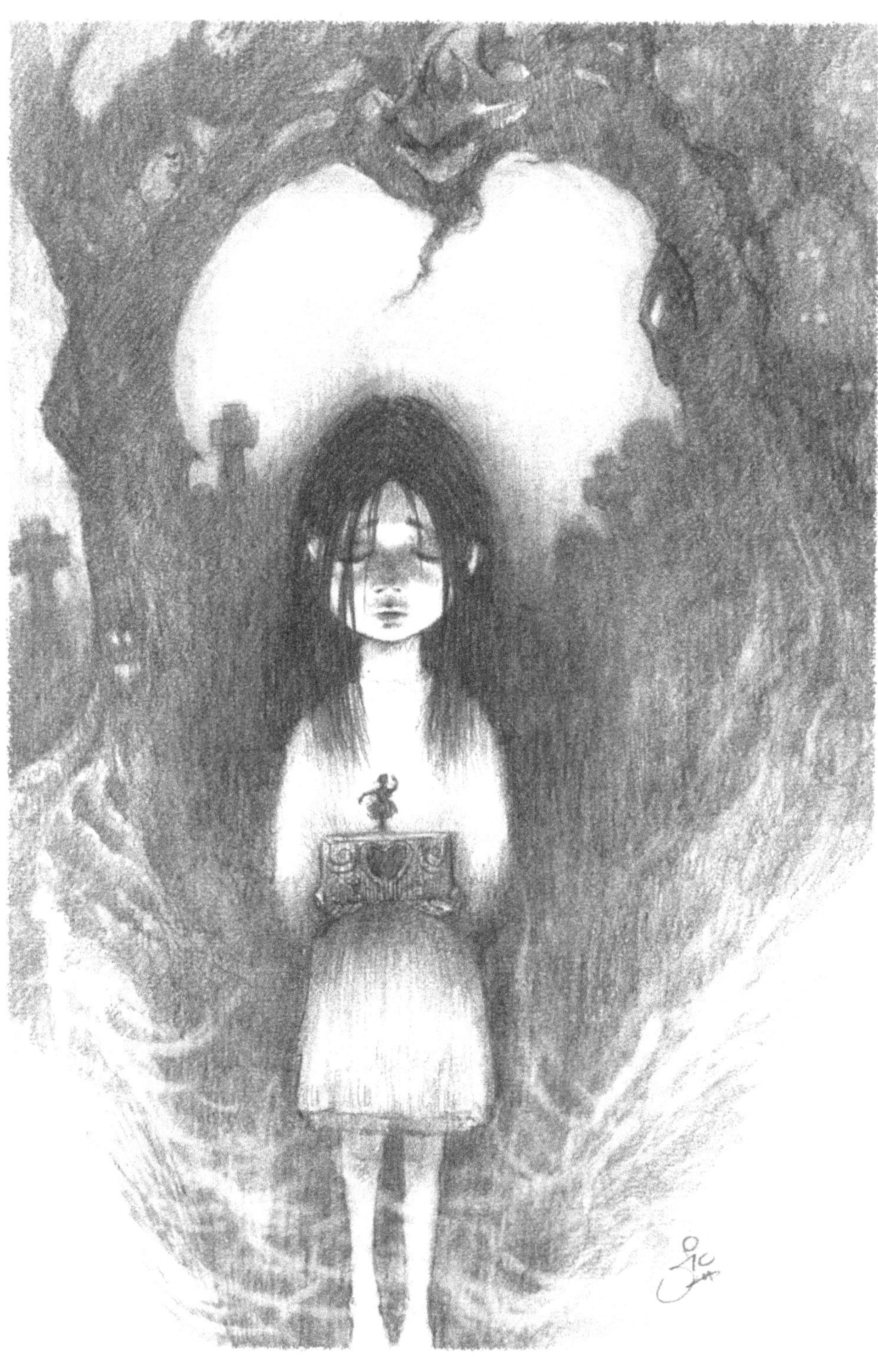

'The Music Box'

THE CURSE OF THE WERECAT

This is a sketch inspired by watching the Universal classic 'The Wolfman' on DVD one evening with my cat Marley on my knee. As often happens, I completed the sketch whilst keeping half an eye on the movie.

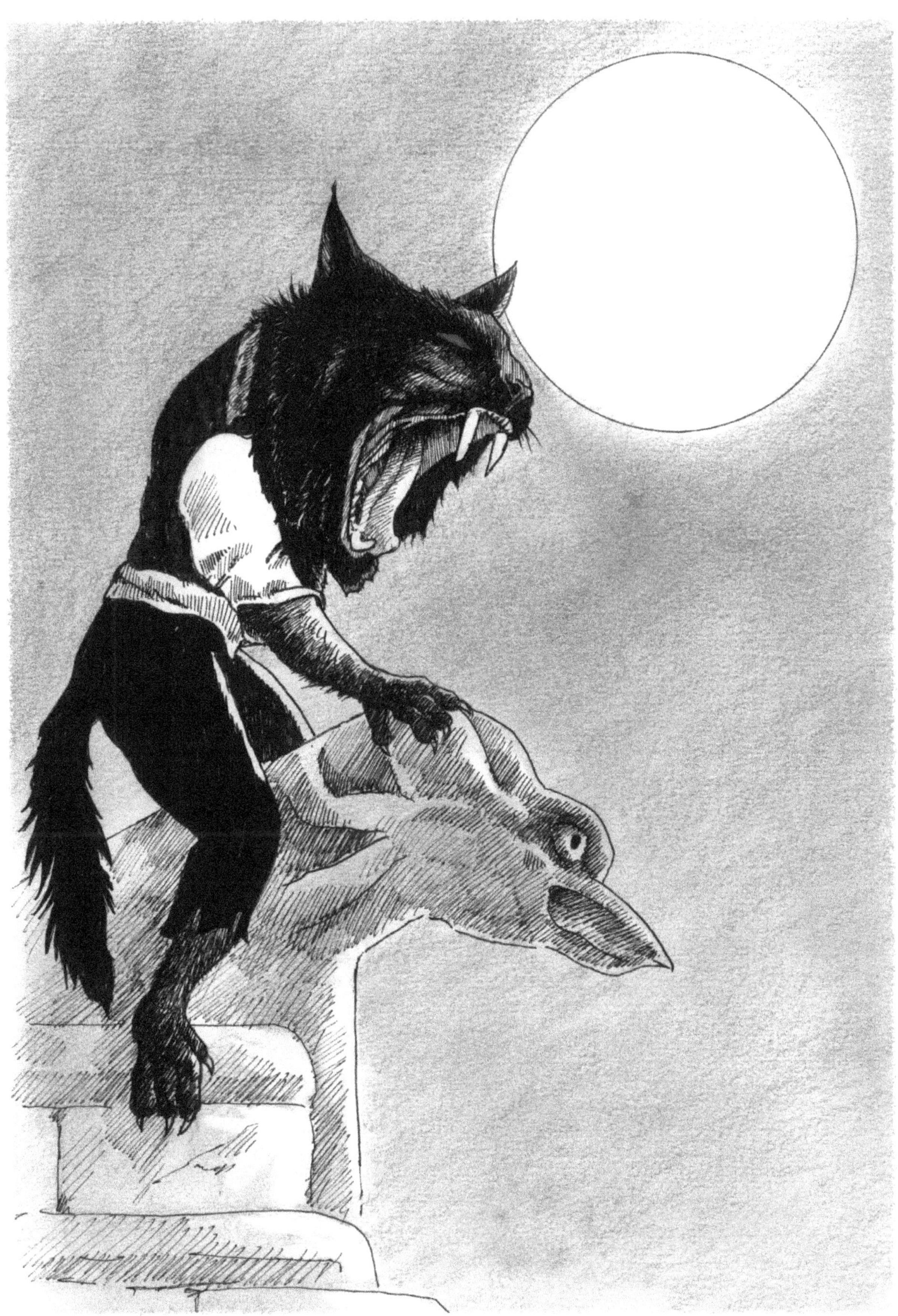

'The Curse of the Werecat'

TEDDY BEAR MONSTERS

Here are another couple of sketches inspired by the old Universal horror movies 'Frankenstein' and 'The Mummy'.

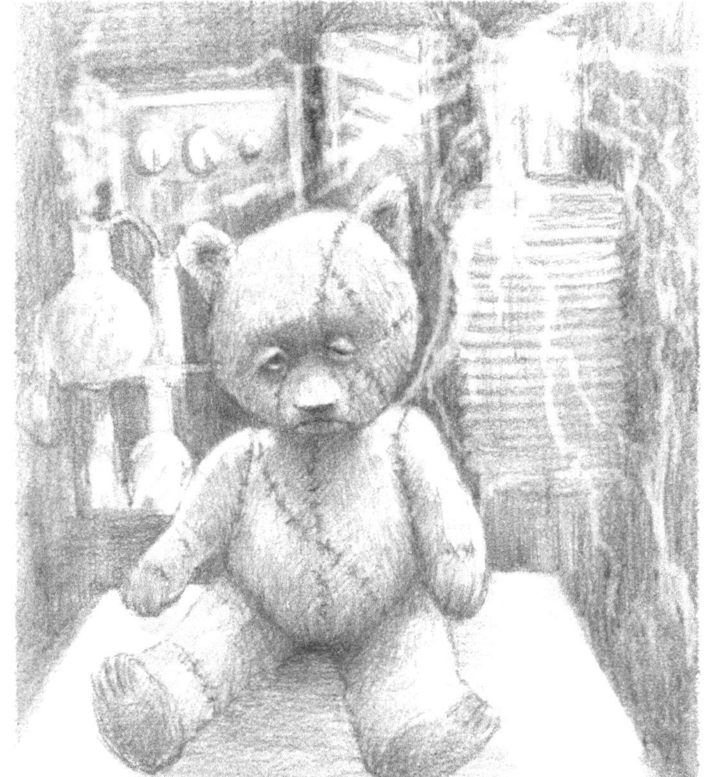

'Frankenstein's Teddy'

The spirit of Boris Karloff lives on in the lifeless (not for long) form of a teddy bear. Why a teddy bear? I have no idea really, apart from the image of a sewn-up bear came to mind once when I watched Boris Karloff playing the monster in 'Frankenstein'.

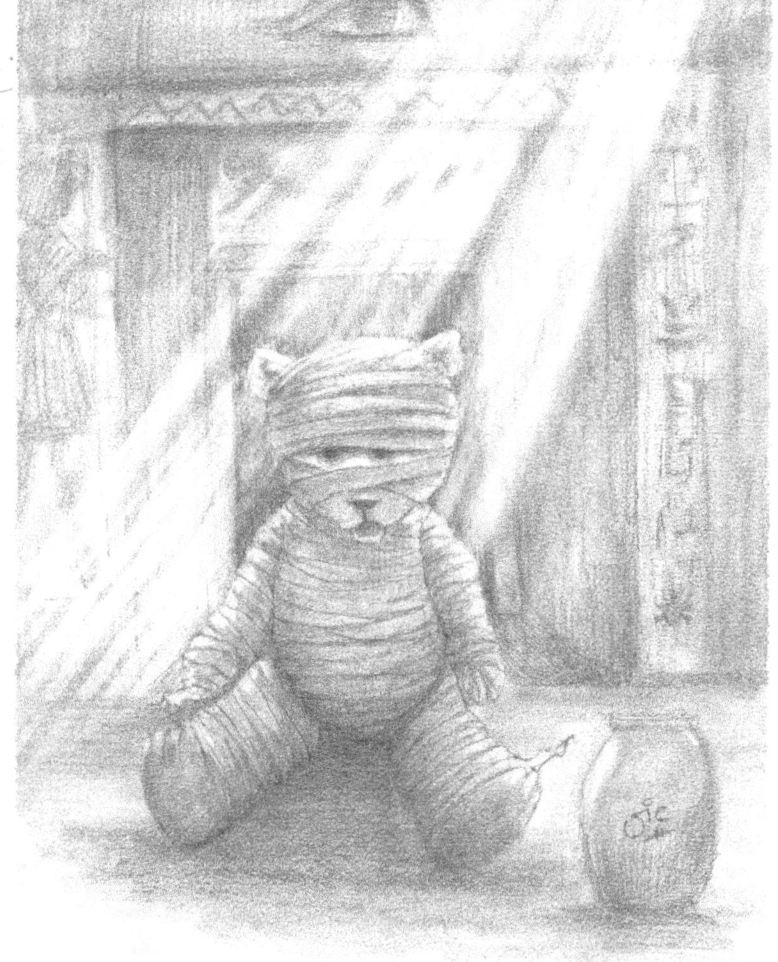

'The Curse of the Teddy's Tomb'

Often, if I have a particular 'theme' in mind, it won't leave me until I have put it on paper.
After 'Frankenstein's Teddy', I immediately got the idea for a series of sketches.
I quickly added this one, more as a reminder to myself to pick up on the 'series' idea at a later date.

LADY MACBETH

I remember reading 'The Scottish Play' at school; in fact, in was part of my English 'O' level exam. I was reminded of it whilst looking through a book of Shakespeare's plays in connection with another book I happened to be working on. This started me thinking about what kind of character Lady Macbeth was and how I visualised her now. This sketch is a long way from being completed, but it served a purpose as one to be filed away for potentially revisiting sometime in the future.

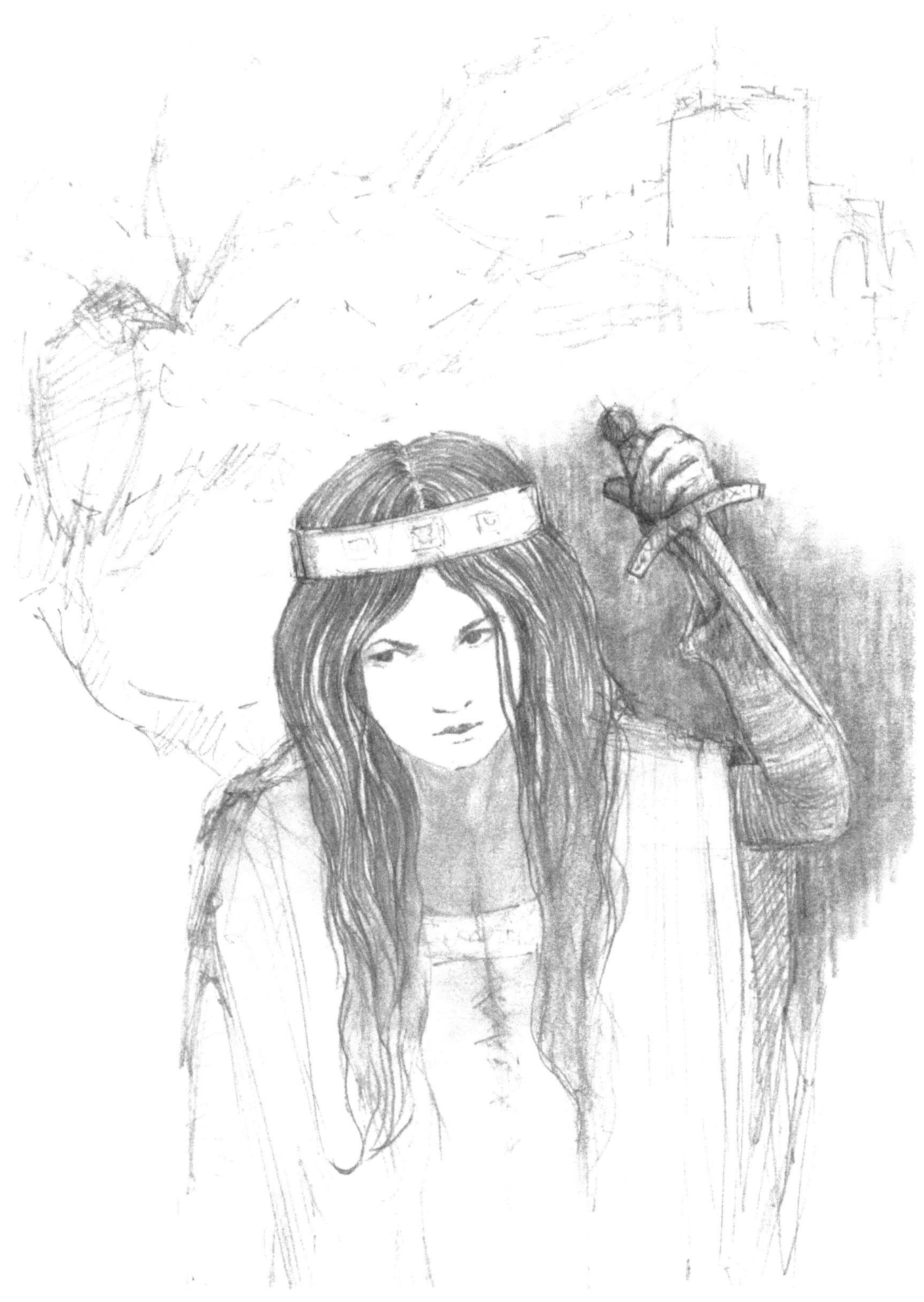

'Lady Macbeth'

'Look like the innocent flower, but be the serpent under it'

JUNGLE BOOK

I'm sure you are aware by now of my love for classic children's stories. In my treasured collection of 'rescued' old books is a 1924 copy of 'The Jungle Books' by Rudyard Kipling, which inspired me as a child, and inspires me still. In 2014 I began a series of Indian ink paintings which were my own interpretations of animal characters from The Jungle Books.

During the period that the Jungle Book stories were still in my mind, I made this ink sketch of one of the wolves from the UK wolf Trust. This was originally a stand-alone sketch to pass a couple of hours in a hotel room. As the sketch progressed, I began to imagine the wolf as Akela, the leader of the wolf pack in the Jungle Book, giving a speech to the rest of the pack on top of the Council Rock. This very same wolf and pose now forms part of a larger Indian ink painting, still in progress at the time of writing, which will become a painting in my 'Jungle Book' series.

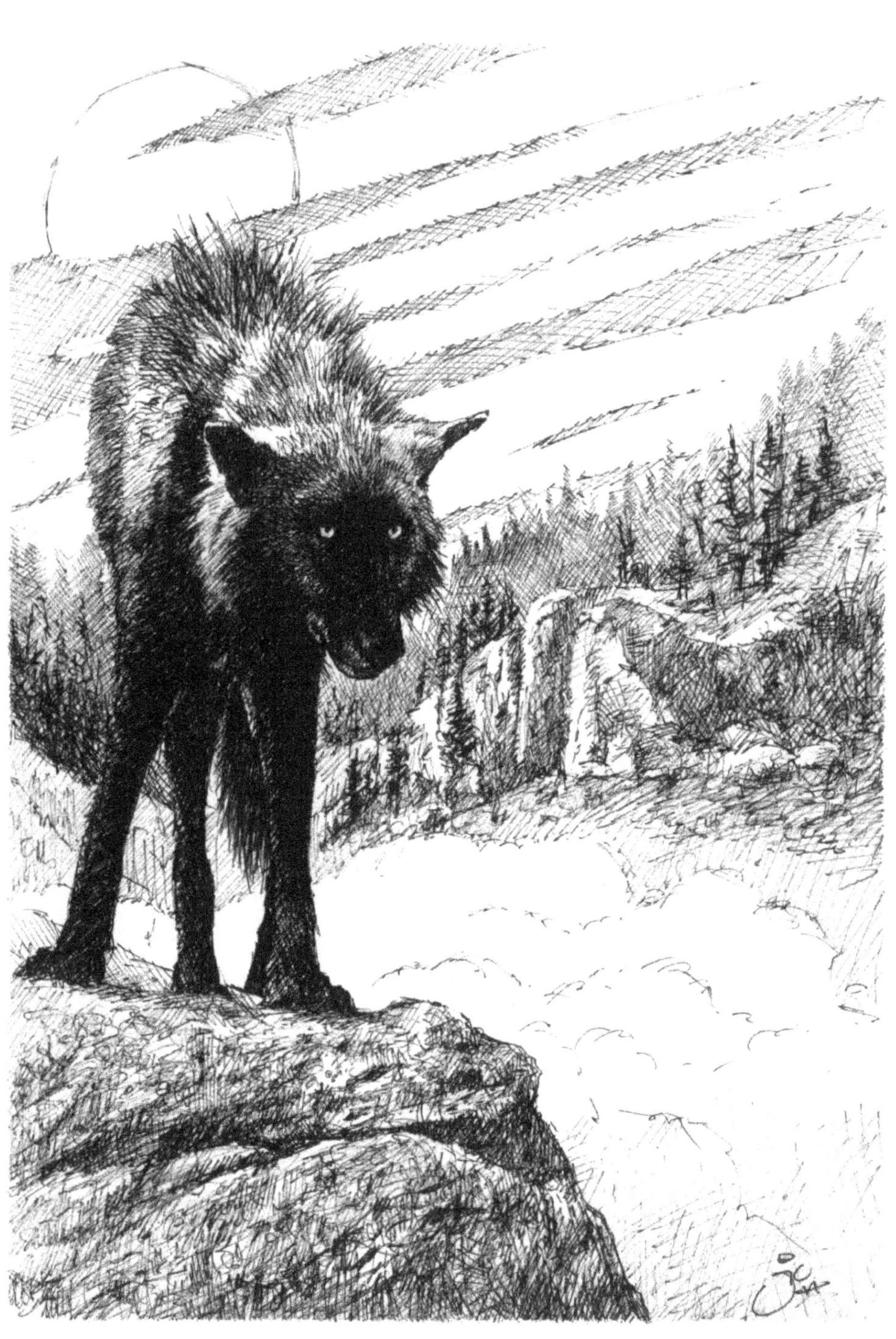

'Black Wolf

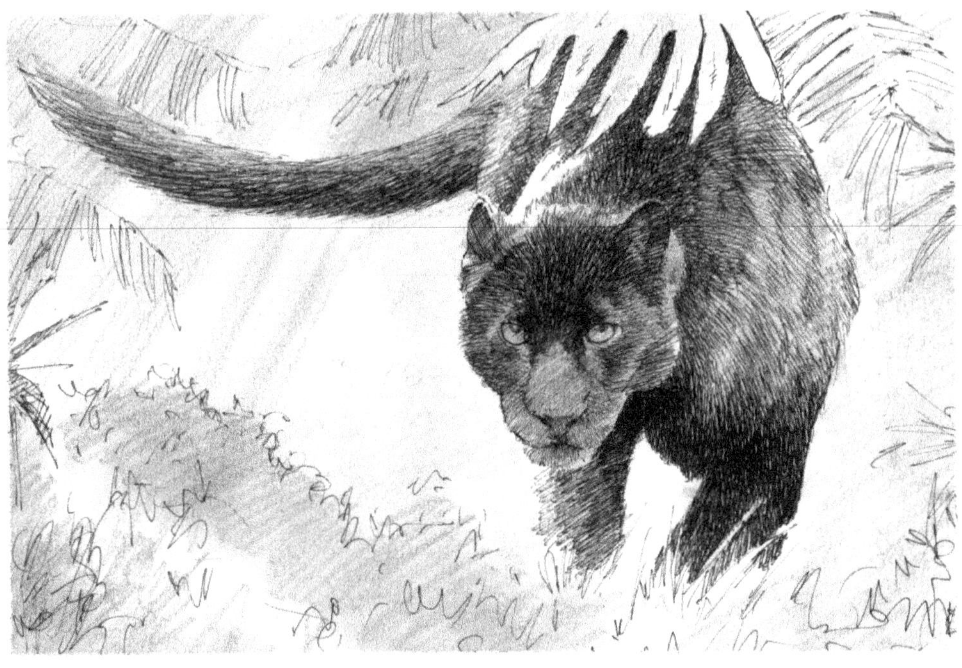

'Bagheera'

The first of my 'Jungle Book' paintings and, indeed, the idea came from an ink pen sketch I made whilst sitting on the sofa, one dull Bank Holiday as 'Ben Hur' was showing on the TV in the background. Before the movie had finished, the 'Bagheera' sketch was complete and the idea for my 'Jungle Book' series was planted firmly in my mind.

'Shere Khan'

Having sketched out the compositional idea for my 'Bagheera' painting, I couldn't wait for more sketching time, either on my own sofa, or sometimes in a hotel. The next character on my list was Shere Khan.

This ink and wash sketch was one of a few that I made to work out a composition for the final Indian ink painting.

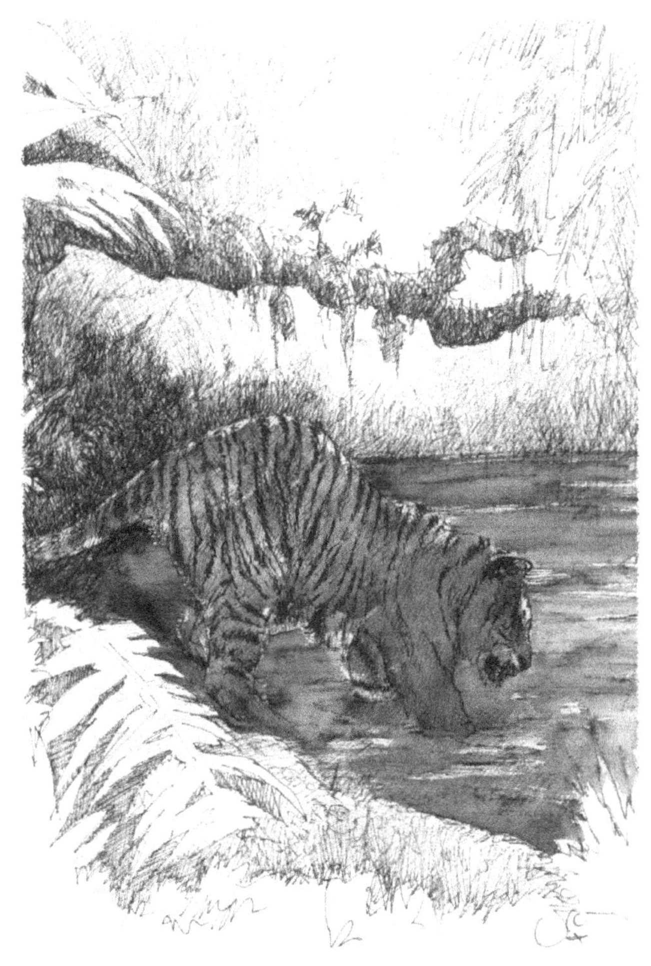

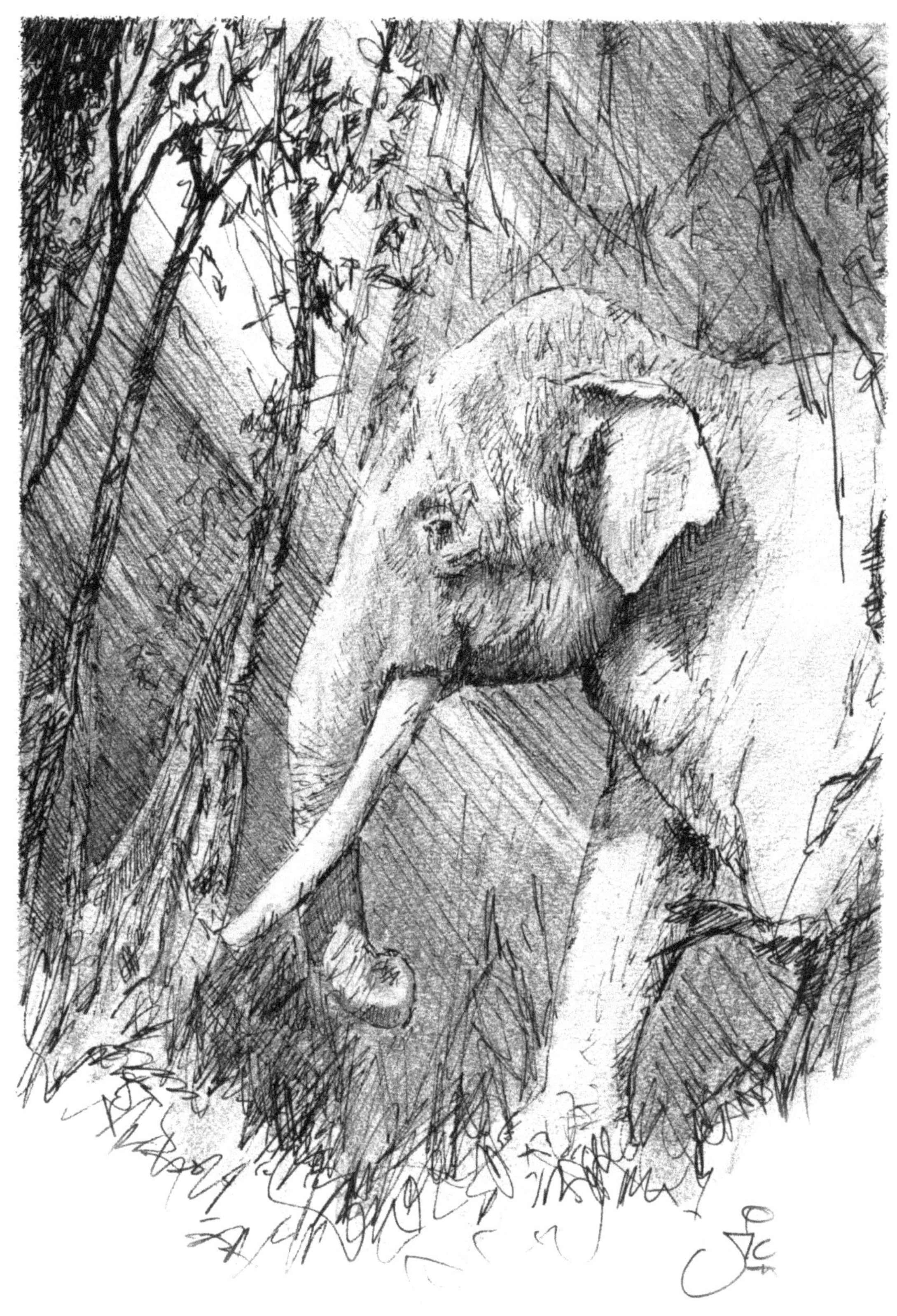

'Elephant'

This was one of those 'multi-purpose' sketches that I sometimes do. Initially the intention was to work out a composition for an ink painting workshop, but, at the same time, it fuelled ideas for another in my 'Jungle Book' series of paintings. I enjoyed playing with the lighting in this one; the effects here achieved with pencil shading over the ink sketch.

BOKRUG

I generally like to draw and paint creatures with fur and feathers, but I was fascinated by a lizard at Marwell Zoo one year, and thought that I should sketch it one day.

That day came in another hotel room somewhere, at around the time I was reading H P Lovecraft, in particular a story about 'Bokrug', the great water lizard.

This was all the inspiration I needed to sketch my Marwell Zoo lizard on a larger scale and in a kind of 'Lovecraftian' setting.

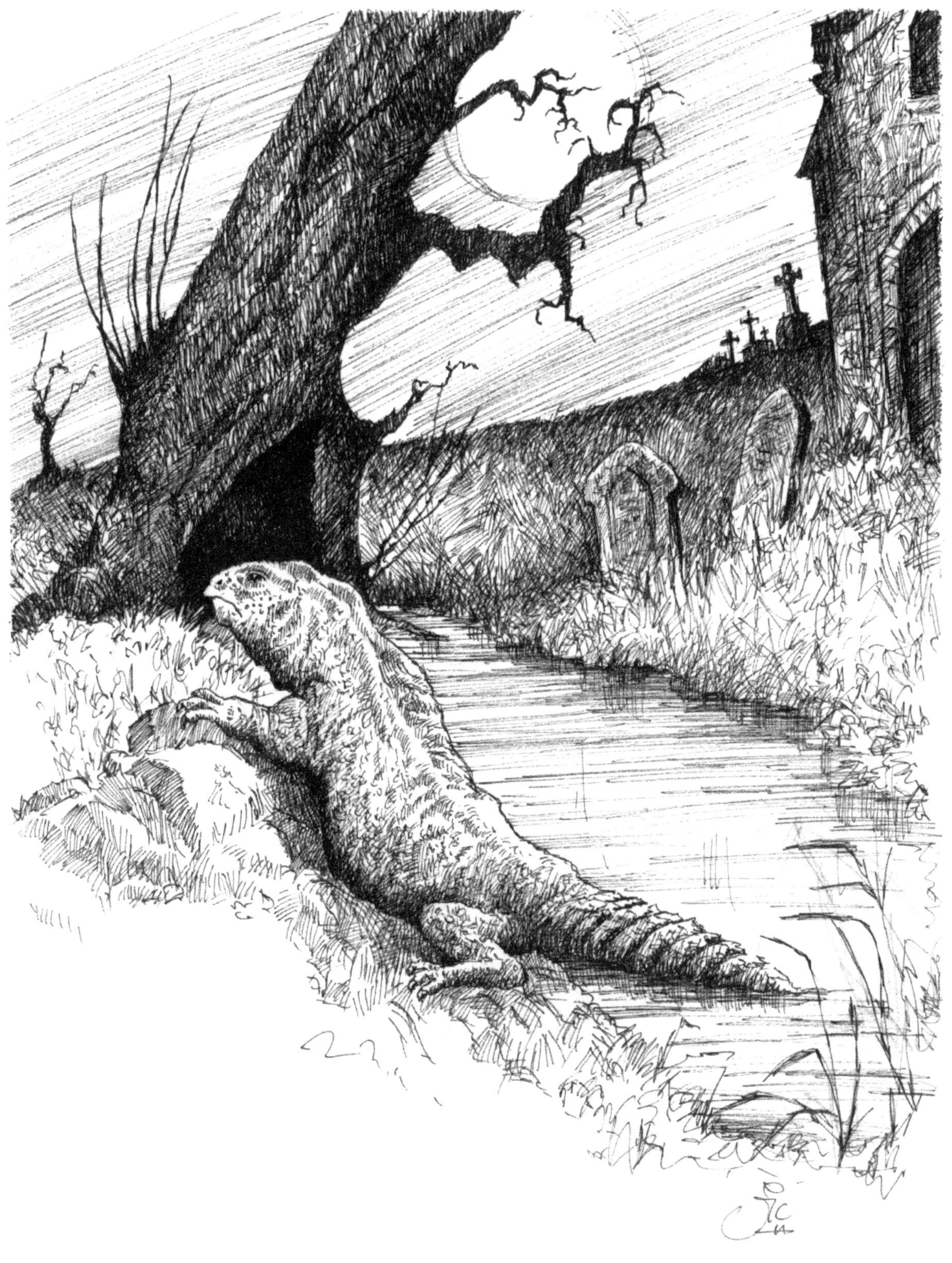

'Bokrug'

DAGON

There is a Lovecraft story about an amphibious deity, Dagon, that rose from the depths to haunt the narrator of the story. Using another Marwell Zoo lizard as reference, a frilled lizard this time, I spent an enjoyable couple of hours in a hotel room creating my visual interpretation of Lovecraft's depiction of Dagon.

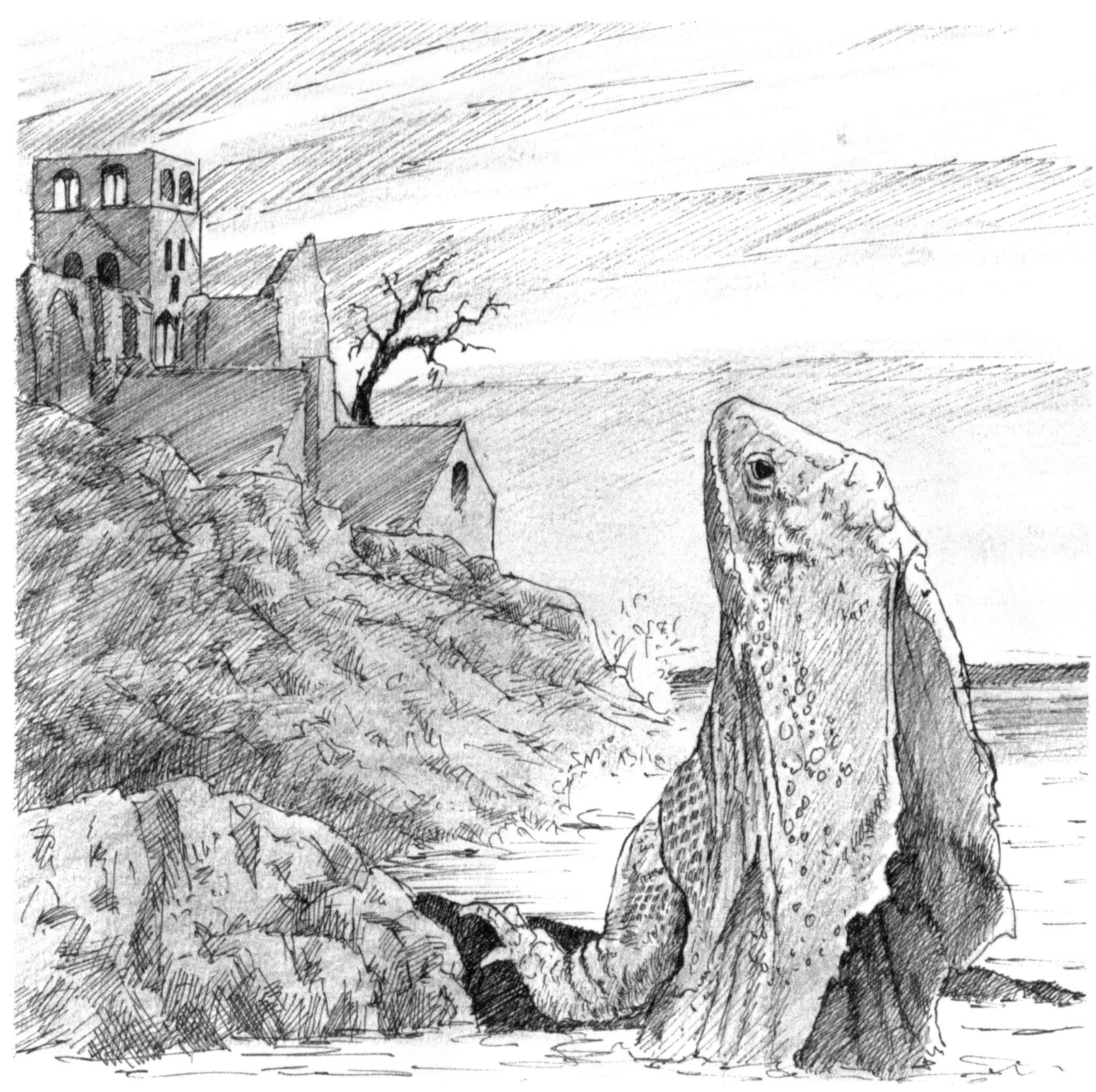

'Dagon'

'With only a slight churning to mark its rise to the surface, the thing slid into view above the dark waters'

THE RAVEN

Ravens have always been a popular subject in Gothic art, alongside cemeteries, churches and so on; all things which fascinate me, in art, literature and film.

I have a couple of Edgar Allan Poe books in my collection, and one of his best narratives for me is 'The Raven'. One evening I was looking through my photos from a holiday in Normandy, and found some of an old abbey and a small village cemetery.

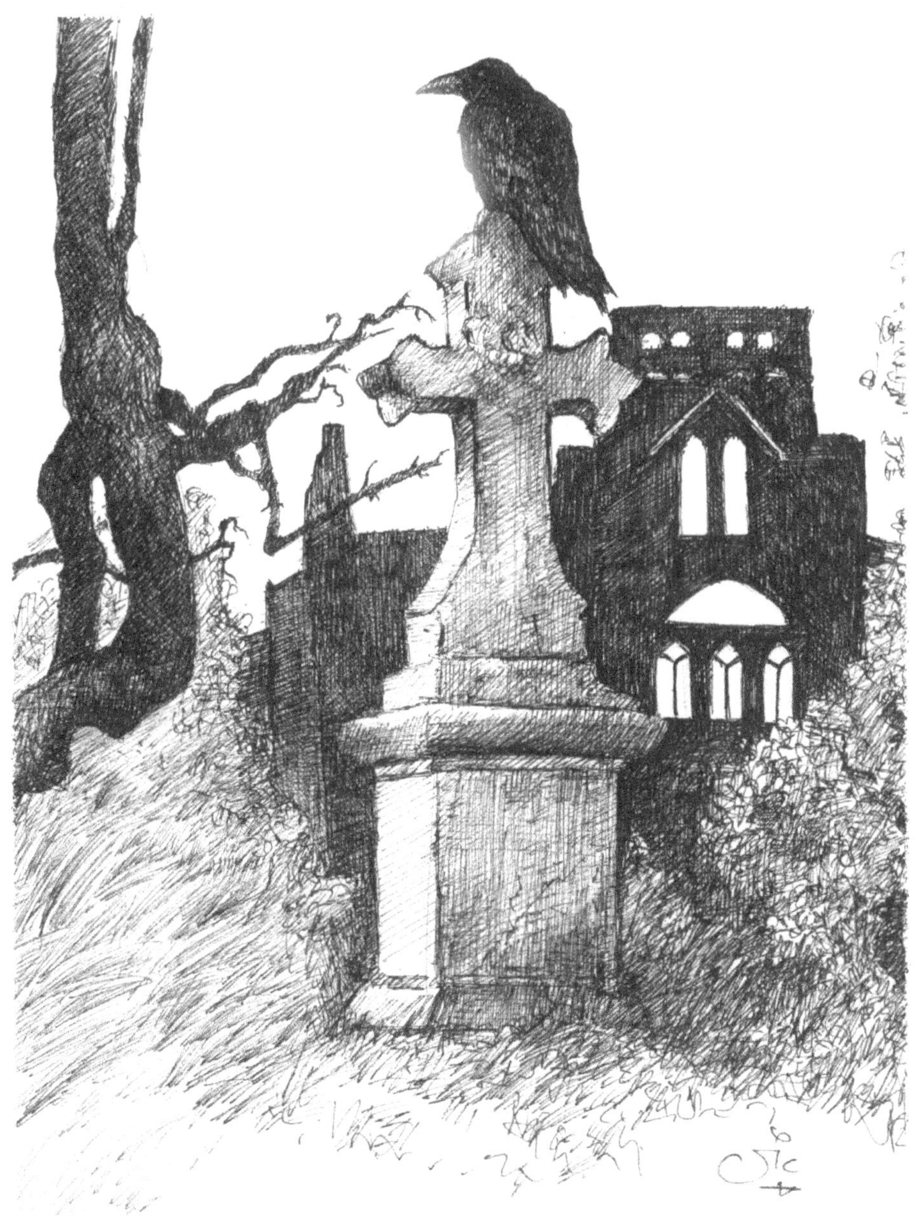

'The Raven'

My initial thought was to combine some of these elements in an ink sketch to pass an hour or two.

Towards the end of the sketch I started thinking about Poe's 'The Raven', and how the bird itself would sit nicely on top of the old stone cross. The addition of an old dead tree to the left completed the scene, which I still enjoy because of the dark atmosphere. I still wonder from time to time just what has caught the raven's attention. Perhaps we'll find out one day!

Fantasy and Mythology

PANDORA

I am a firm believer in learning from those who have gone before; artists traditionally learning from old masters is a prime example. There are many artists and illustrators whose work I admire and, indeed, have influenced me over many years.

One of those artists is J W Waterhouse, the post Pre-Raphaelite painter; especially when it comes to his 'mythological' paintings.

As many have done before me, I sometimes find it a useful warm-up exercise to sketch from a sculpture or favourite artist's painting. In the case of Waterhouse, this can help me to develop my own Pre-Raphaelite style sketches.

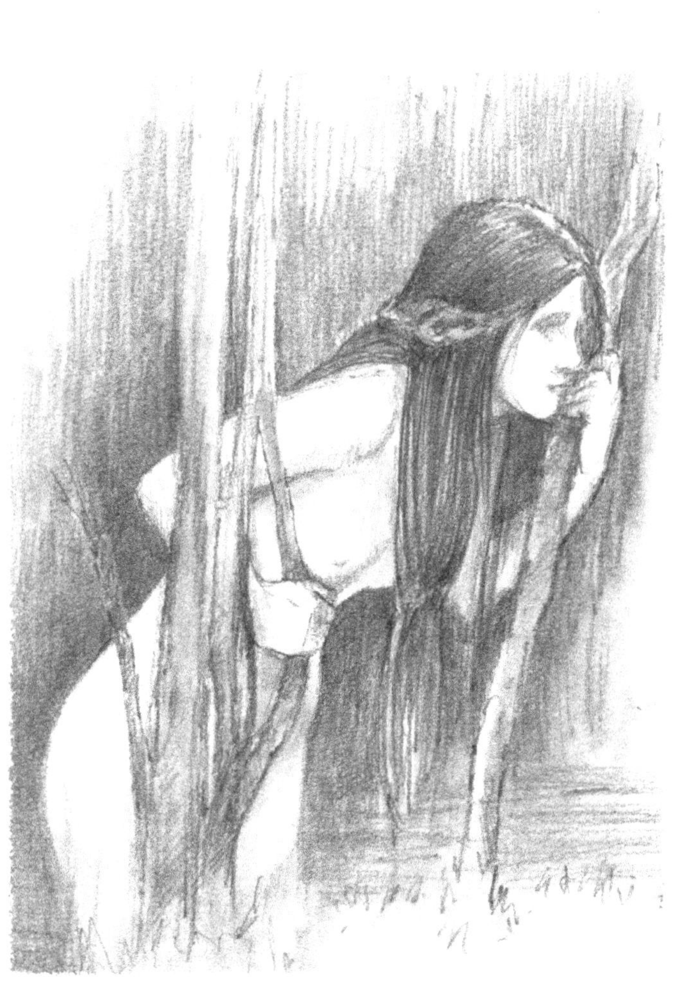

'A Naiad'

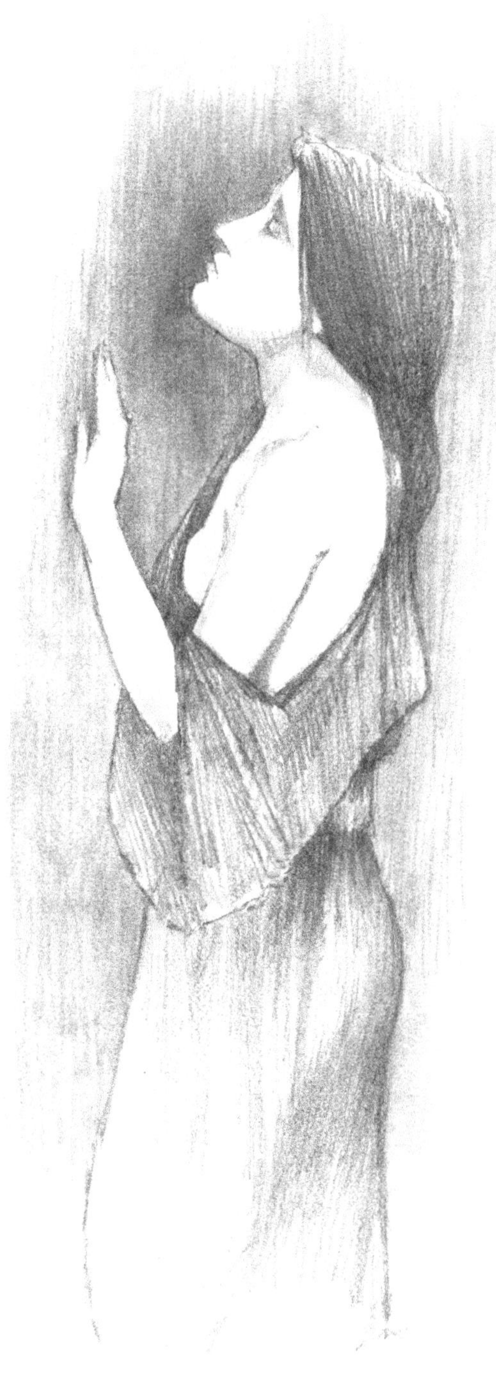

'Pandora'

The first two sketches in this section are in recognition of Waterhouse's influence, sketched details from his paintings of 'Pandora' and 'A Naiad'.

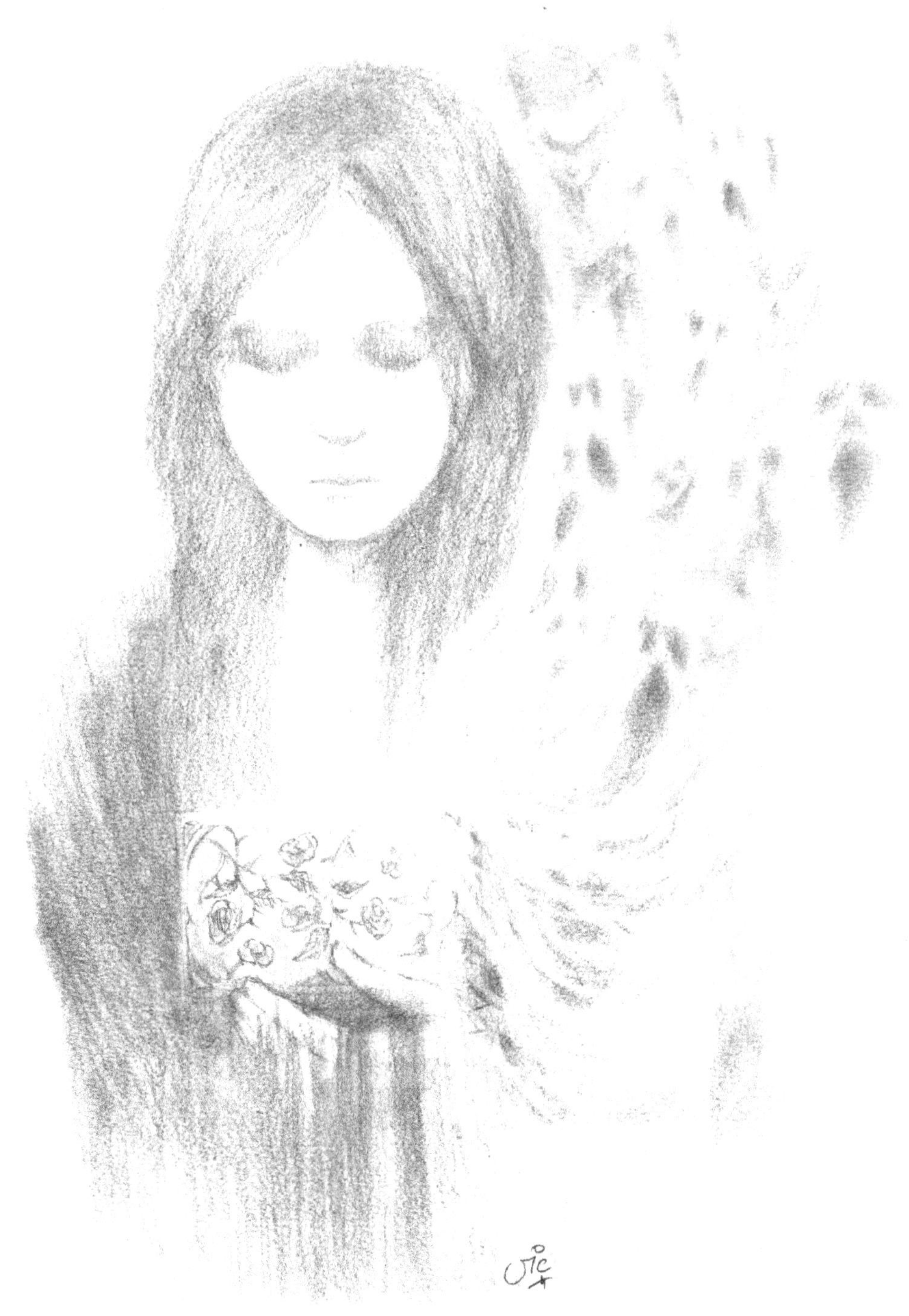

'Pandora's Box'

This sketch was undoubtedly influenced by J W Waterhouse's 'Pandora', but I wanted to create a more ethereal look to my version. I had the idea of the box that held all the evils let out into the world being the only part of the sketch in focus. Pandora's face and figure are less detailed, almost suggested, with a downward look to try and convey her feelings as she realises what she has just done.

Then I had fun trying to illustrate the evils being released, again with suggestion rather than detail. I eventually did this by sketching the general form with the side of a pencil and using an eraser to 'reverse sketch' the faces.

At around the same time as I sketched 'Pandora's Box', and enjoying the ethereal look to that sketch, I did a quick sketch of 'Summer', intended as a pre-illustration sketch for a series illustrating the four seasons (see the other three in the 'doodles' section). I wanted to portray a feeling of hazy summer heat in the sketch, so decided that it shouldn't therefore be too detailed. Equally, the tones were important to convey stronger summer lighting.

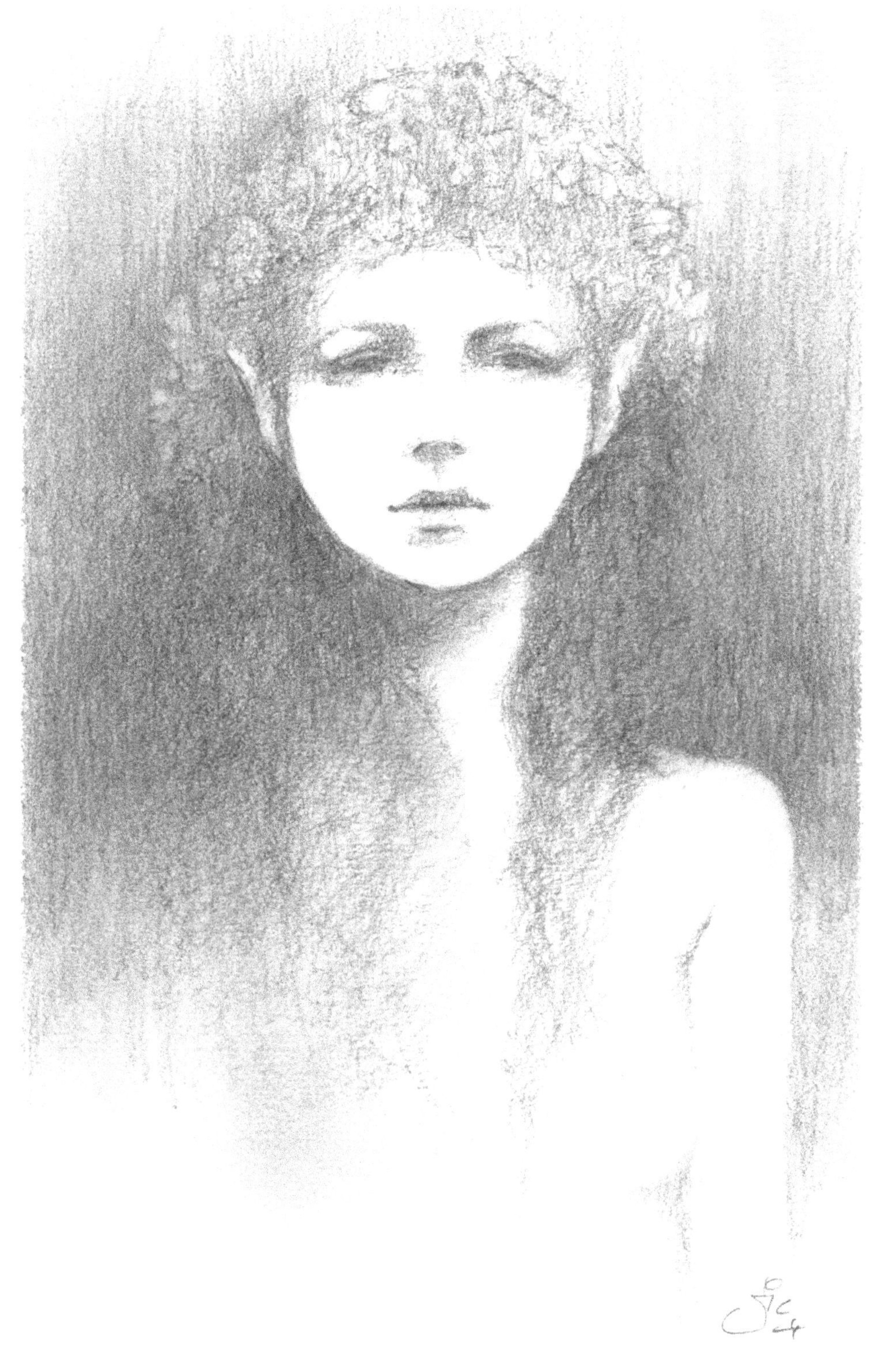

'Summer'

PAN

On top of the old corn exchange building in Newark-On Trent are a couple of statues. One of them, 'Plenty', is of an old, bearded man holding a cornucopia, or horn of plenty, a symbol of abundance.
One evening, as I sat down to watch one of my favourite films, 'Pan's Labyrinth', I remembered the statue, and thought that with the additions of ram's horns and ears, he could be a model for the 'Great God Pan', which was to be one of the ink illustrations in my book 'Dark Angels'.

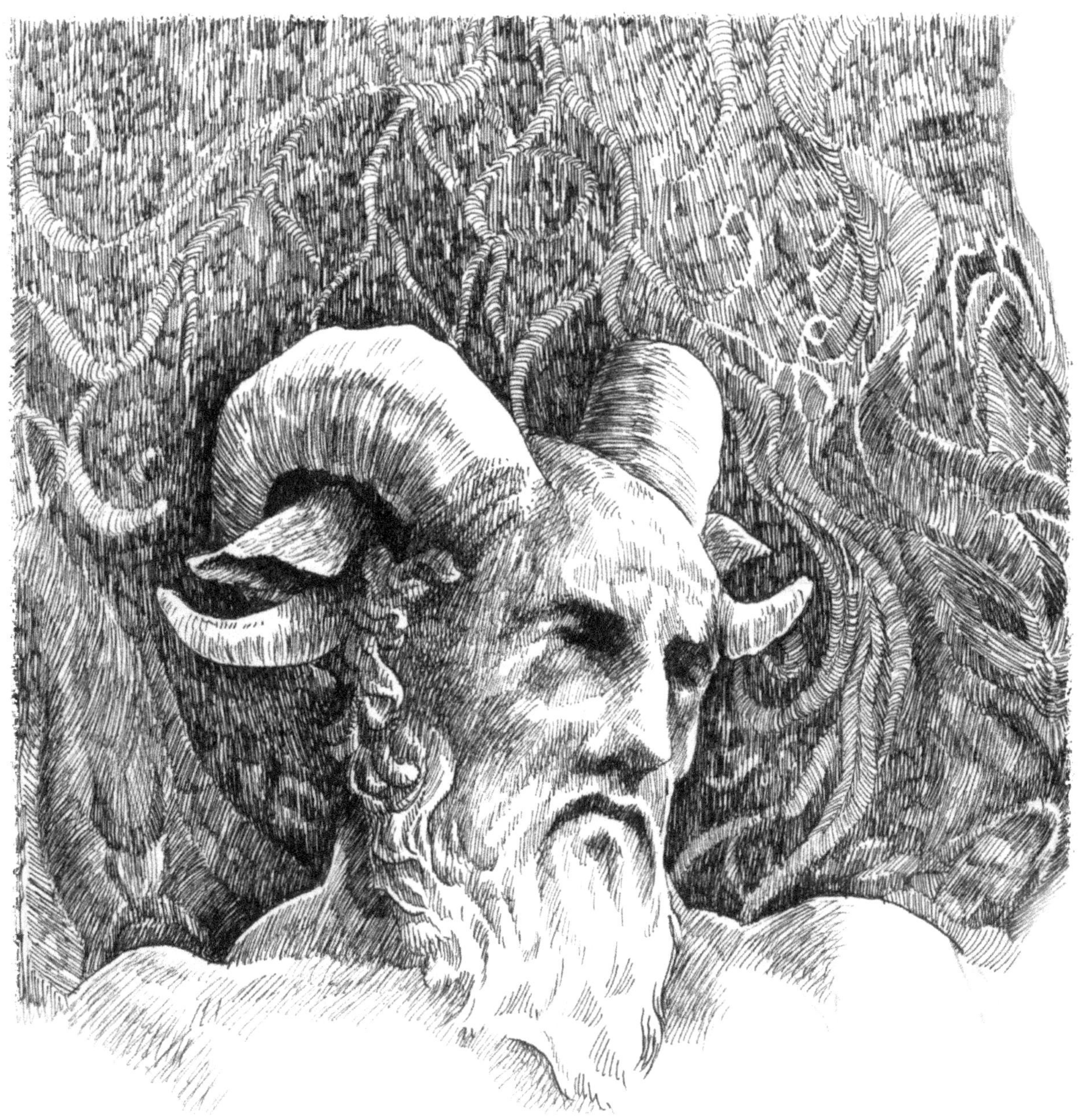

'Pan'

Having sketched Pan's head with an ink pen, I noticed that the Faun, or Pan, in the film lived underground; the walls of his lair made up of cold, damp earth and exposed tree roots.
This became the inspiration for textured ink doodling in the background of my sketch. As always, this part turned into a fun exercise in texturing, trying to capture the atmosphere in the film, and even including some 'hidden' faces among the twisted roots.

BANSHEE

A familiar figure in Irish folklore is the banshee. It is one of those creatures that has undergone many interpretations; I even remember watching a pretty awful film about one a long time ago.
More recently, I discovered a poem by Francis Duggan about a banshee, which immediately cemented an image in my head that needed to be sketched in order to cast it out!
Here are a few of Duggan's lines that really inspired me:

'As the moon at midnight moves through the starry sky
Out there in the bog land the Banshee's shrill cry
The one seldom heard and that human eyes cannot see'

Some say that the banshee can take on the appearance of a beautiful young woman, often with straggly dark hair. So this was my starting point for the sketch. Nevertheless, I still wanted my banshee to convey an evil spirit, so the black eyes seemed to work well. The addition of a full moon hiding behind the dark trees, and use of a kneadable eraser to create a mist rising from the bog managed to complete the image that I had in my head after reading the verse.

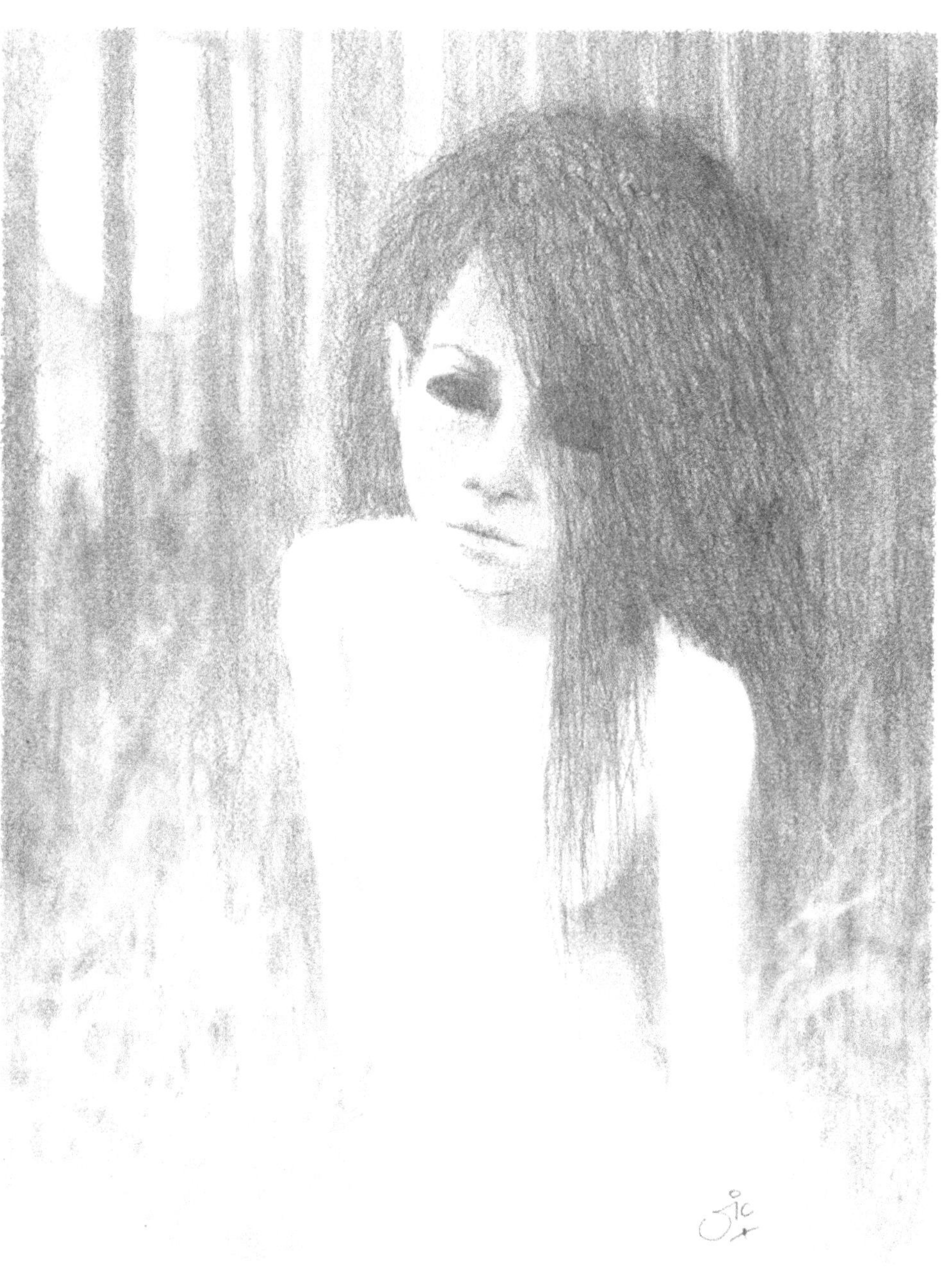

'Banshee'

THE FOUNTAIN OF SALMACIS

In late summer there was a large cluster of oyster mushrooms growing in Bunny Wood. I thought I might go back with a sharp knife the following day and pick some to eat.
When I looked at the photographs I took of the mushrooms later that day, I couldn't help noticing that the whole cluster, which was quite large, looked like an elaborate fountain. I imagined a fairy bathing in a pool beneath the waters cascading down from each of the large mushroom trumpets.
Then I remembered a song by the band Genesis from way back in the 70s, called 'The Fountain of Salmacis', based on the Greek myth of Salmacis, who basically was a lazy Naiad (see verse below). The mushrooms could surely become the Naiad's fountain for her to bathe in.

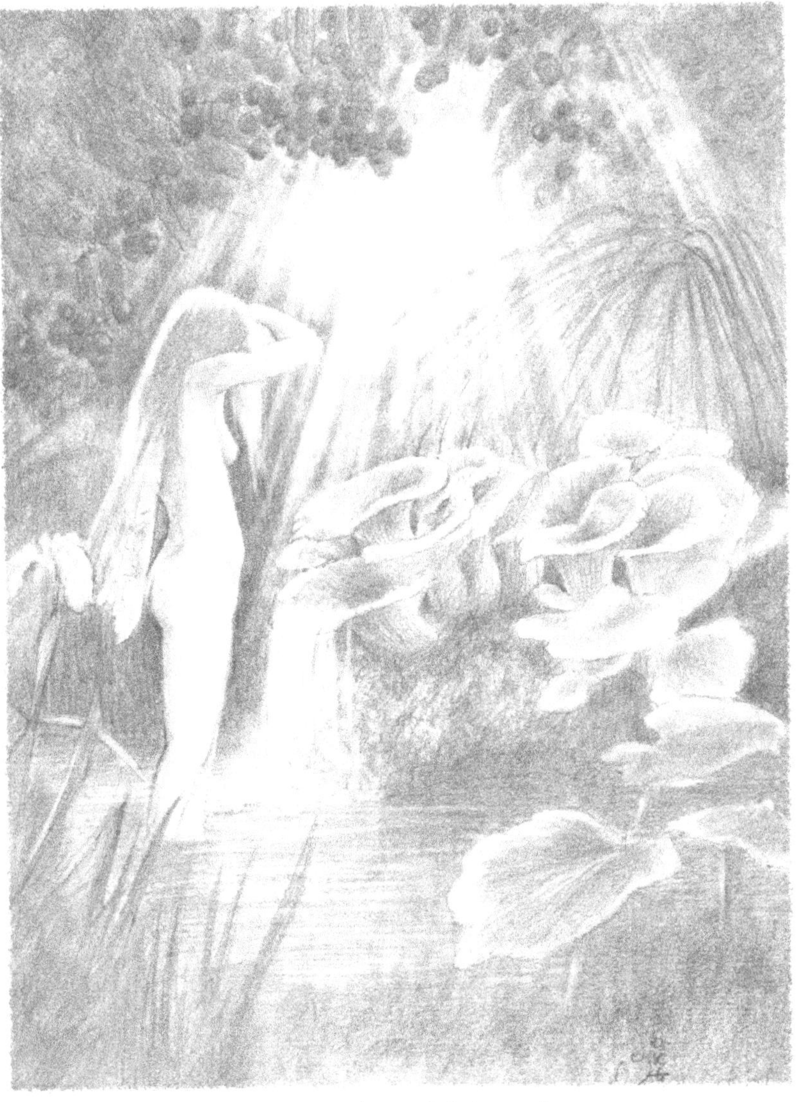

'The Fountain of Salmacis'

**"There dwelt a Nymph, not up for hunting or archery:
unfit for footraces. She the only Naiad not in Diana's band.
Often her sisters would say: "Pick up a javelin, or
bristling quiver, and interrupt your leisure for the chase!"
But she would not pick up a javelin or arrows,
nor trade leisure for the chase.
Instead she would bathe her beautiful limbs and tend to her hair,
with her waters as a mirror."**

Although the sketch was completed over a couple of evenings, I didn't tire of it as there were so many different elements to play with. The naiad Salmacis had to be miniaturised to make sense of the mushroom fountain, so she became a fairy instead. Large foliage in the foreground and clusters of berries overhead helped in reducing the whole scene.
By far my favourite part of this sketch was using a kneadable eraser to achieve almost magical lighting effects; the sunbeams, cascading water and most of all the glowing highlights in the fairy's hair and wings.
I often wonder about turning this into a full colour illustration or even a painting. Then again, part of me thinks that I might not be able to capture the atmosphere of the original, non-pressured sketch.

TROLLS AND TREES

Like many of us, I've always had a fascination for tales of trolls living in deep, dark forests; perhaps it's down to our partly Nordic ancestry.
One of the greatest illustrators of such stories was John Bauer, a Swedish artist who, along with his wife and son, died tragically young. Nevertheless, he left behind a body of work that I never tire of looking at.
Bauer's portrayals of trolls and dark forests are so evocative, making you want to delve deeper, even though you probably shouldn't!

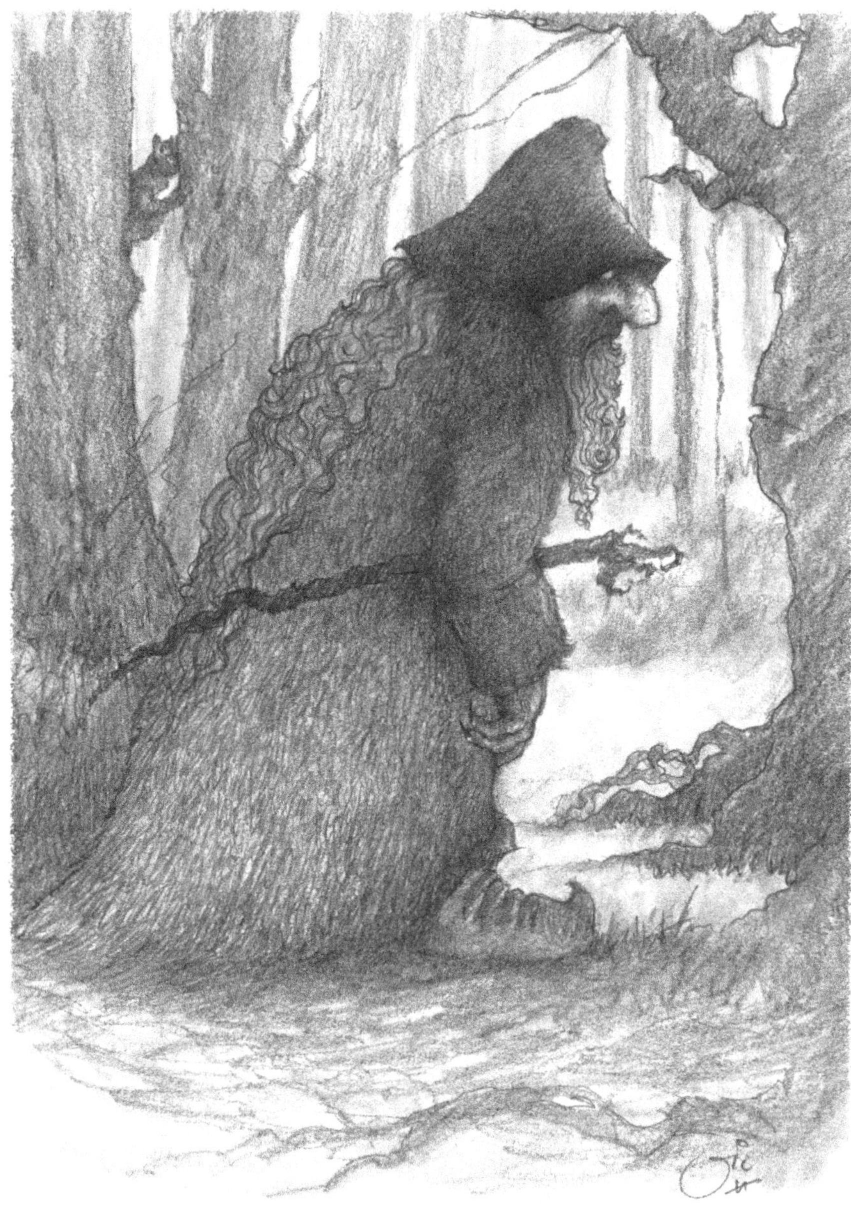

'The Squirrel Troll'

Not far from my home is a place we call 'The Big Wood', where we often walk our dogs. Sometimes, I will go there by myself and wander off the pathways, and enter a world of old dead trees, bramble thickets and carpets of pine needles. Now and again there will be a tree that has been blown down by strong winds, exposing huge root balls that take on mysterious dark shapes.
One such root ball caught my attention, and as I got nearer I could see the shape of a stooping figure; it had to be a troll! In the sketch I made later that evening, the troll came to life, complete with a stick that he uses to catch squirrels.
You might just make out Peanut the squirrel hiding on a branch in the background. Trolls can sometimes be found taking the form of trees.
Whenever I'm out walking in Bunny Wood or the Big Wood I see evidence of tree trolls. Generally these trolls conceal themselves well, hiding their faces so that only in certain light will their features be seen to those who know what they are looking for.

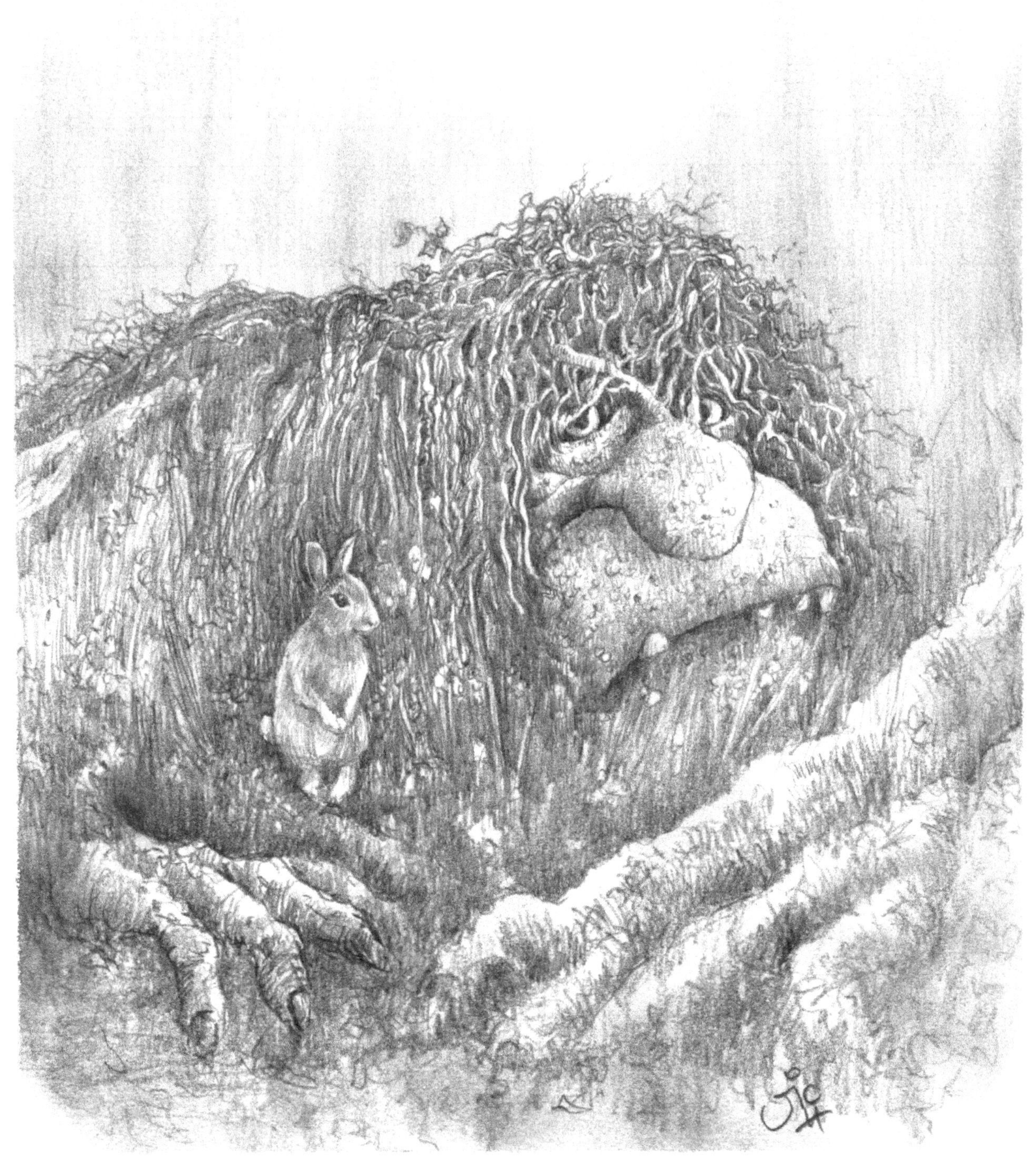

'Slumbering Troll'

This troll has been asleep for a very long time, for they can be rather lazy creatures. At the arrival of spring, the troll is awakened by a young rabbit that has been nibbling at wildflowers and leaves growing in his straggly, root-like hair. This was a really fun sketch to do, creating a living creature out of an exposed root ball, from a tree long since toppled by the wind. The idea of the 'tormenting' young rabbit and, perhaps, a little story, came about halfway through the sketch, and so had to be included.

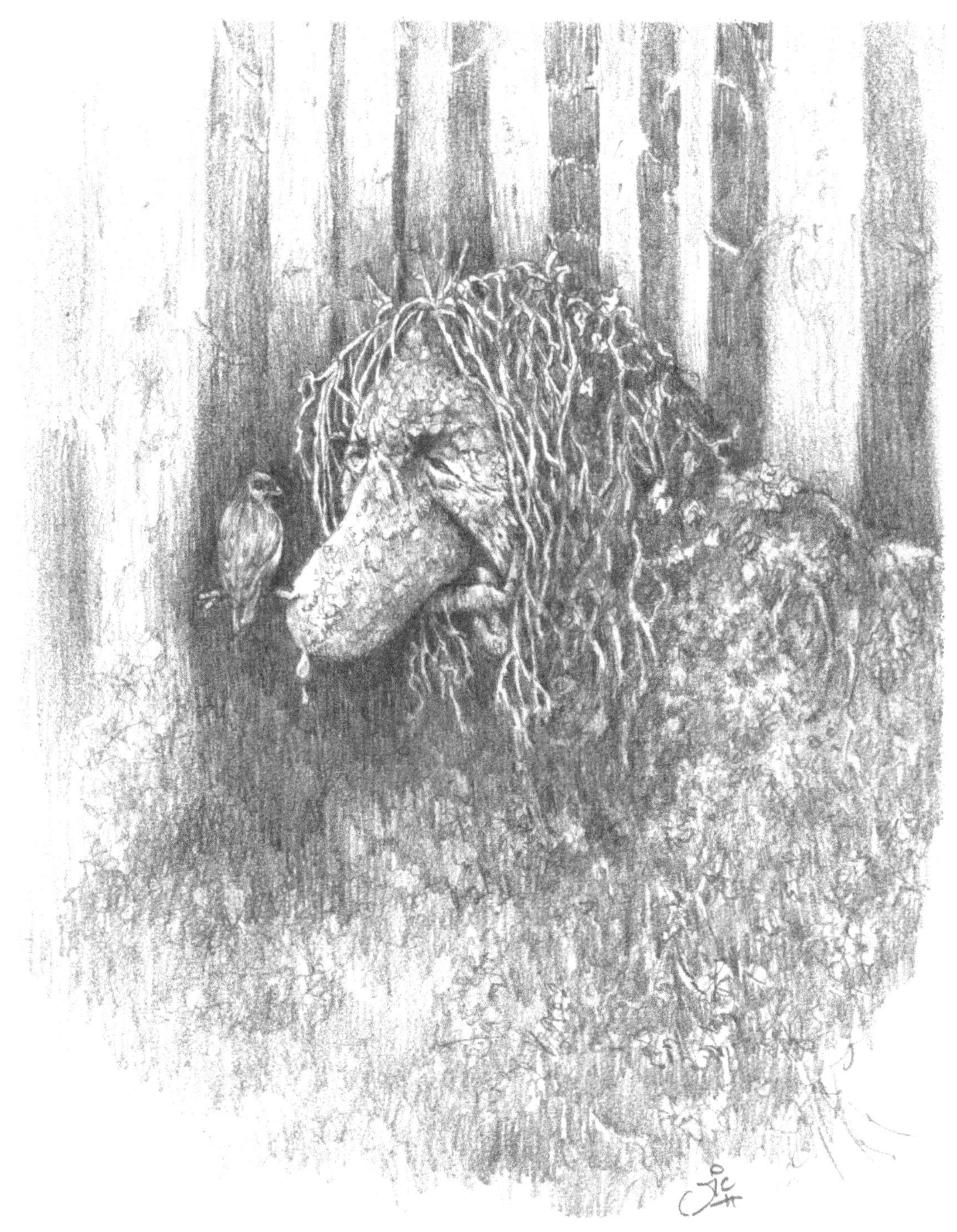

'Petrified Troll'

Occasionally a tree troll can sleep for so long that it begins to petrify, becoming a part of the tree in which it is hiding. Such is the case with the 'Petrified Troll'. Unable to move after waking up, he can only watch helplessly as ivy grows from his hair, moss covers his body and his skin turns to lichen-covered bark.
The uncomfortable feeling the troll has with sap dripping from his nose is only made worse by a cheeky sparrow perching on a branch growing out of it.
This sketch reflects my love of John Bauer's artwork. The trees in the Big Wood remind me of the forest backgrounds in Bauer's illustrations, tall and straight with dark spaces in between.

'Tree Devil'

The 'Tree Devil' was discovered in Bunny Wood one morning. There was a tree stump with a vaguely human profile and what looked to me like a twisted horn growing down one side.
With not too many changes to the photograph I took, the Tree Devil began to come to life in this quick but satisfying sofa sketch. Certainly one to keep for a future illustration and/or story reference. I love looking for faces in old trees.
Sometimes the face can only be seen in a certain light, or from a particular angle. Whenever I find a face, friendly or otherwise, I cannot wait to create a sketch and bring it to life.

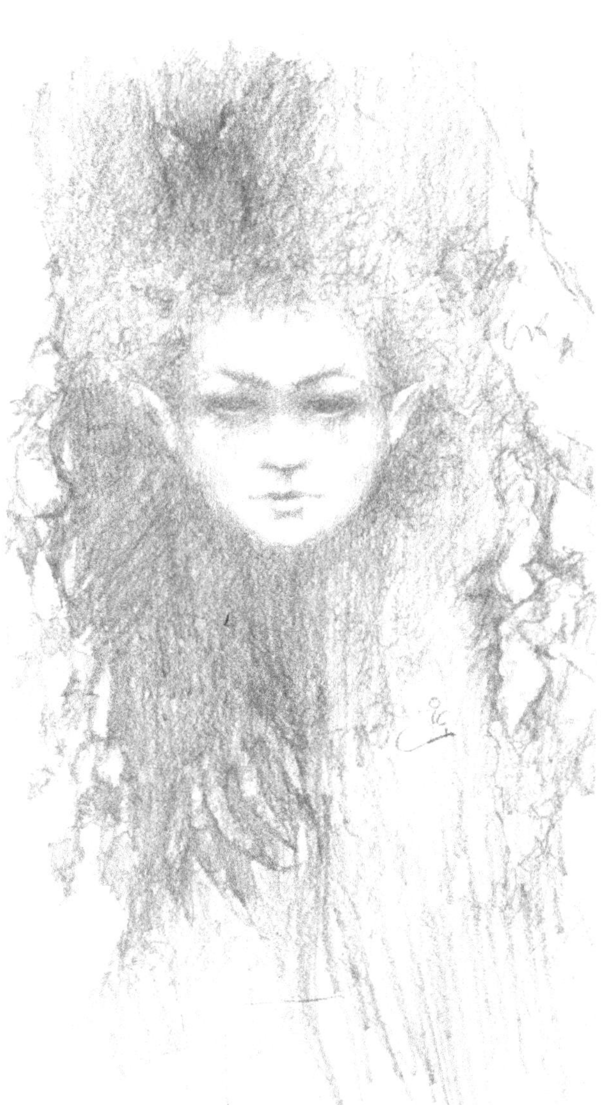

'Tree Sprite'

The 'Tree Sprite' began as a character doodle for some kind of sprite or male fairy. After a while the tree grew around the face, as a result of my wanting to add some darker shading; these things just happen sometimes when you're doodling.

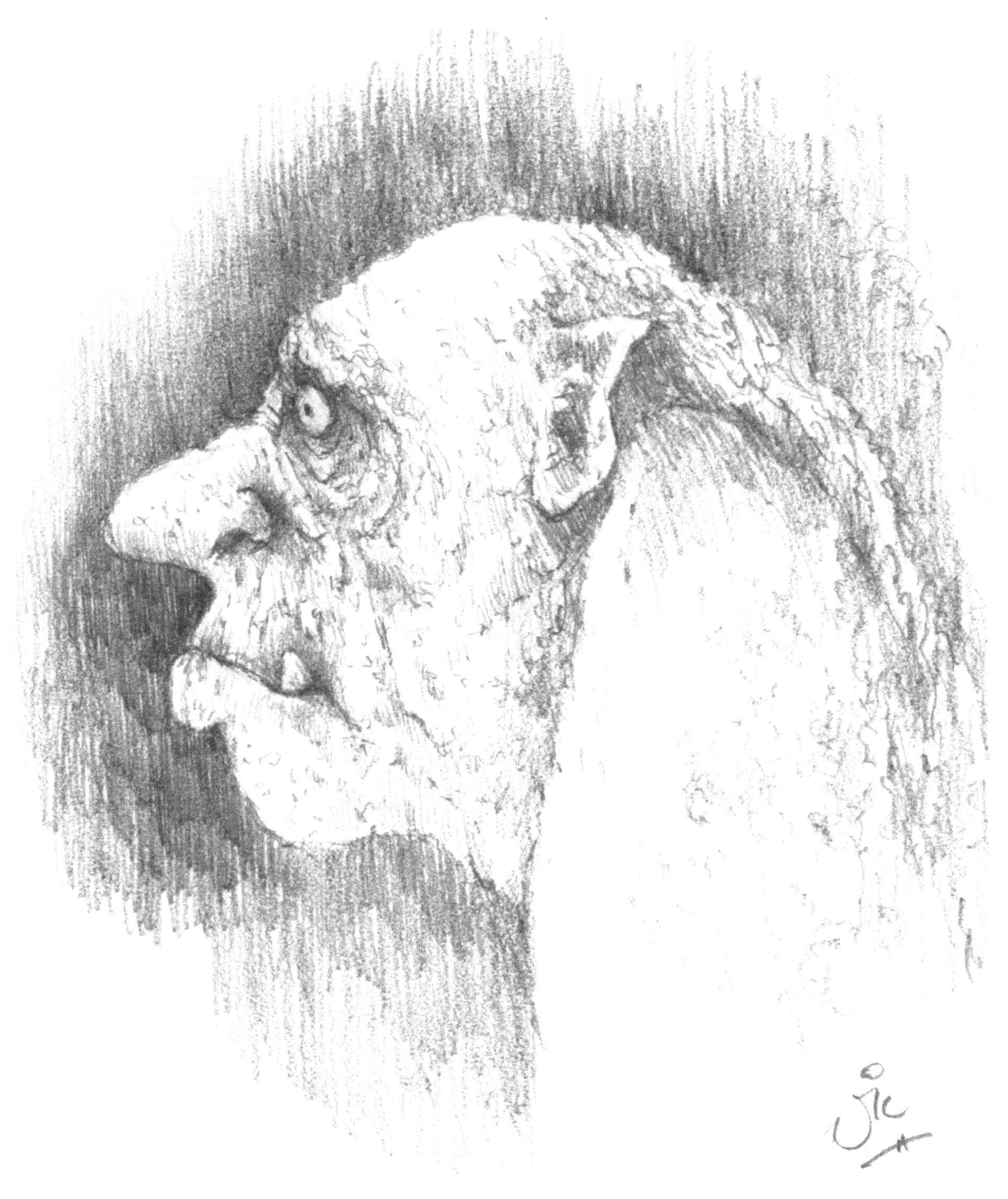

'Old Tree Troll'

Following on from the 'Tree Devil', which pretty much created itself from the photograph I took, I decided to create a tree troll from scratch.

Using techniques and textures I was now familiar with, and having looked at a huge amount of trees, I found that this sketch of an old tree troll came to life very quickly. I did try a few different expressions, but as I had already created the 'devil', I wanted this troll to have a stooped posture and a face that, perhaps once scary, was now one to be pitied.

Fairies, Nymphs and Witches

FAIRIES

In the book of short stories that I have also been working on, even as I write this, there are woodland creatures, fairies and other characters. There are, I'm sure, fairy attributes that we are all familiar with; after all they are pretty much a part of most children's upbringing.

Fairies have wings, unless they are very unfortunate. To paraphrase J M Barrie, fairies can be either good or bad, but they are too small to be both at the same time. They can be dressed or undressed; fairies don't necessarily have the same moral or social hang-ups that humans do.

There can be fairies for all manner of natural things; fruit fairies, flower fairies, tree fairies and so on.

All of that means, of course, that we are at liberty to create images of fairies as we see fit, or as befits the situation; and so sketching fairies has become one of my more enjoyable evening pastimes.

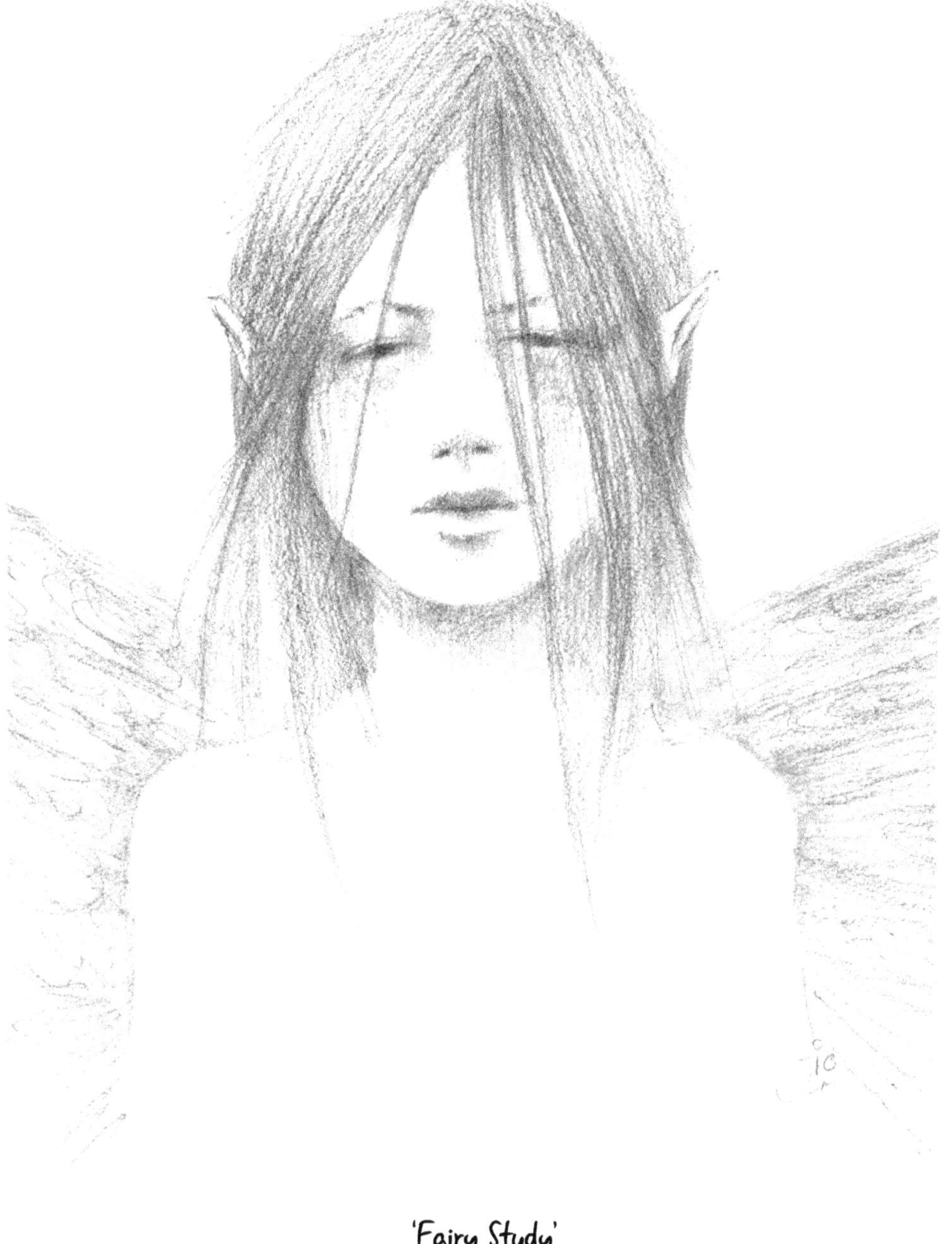

'Fairy Study'

Having previously enjoyed sketching Tinker Bell in a bit of a huff, I decided that I rather like fairies with a bit of attitude, rather than them being far too sweet little creatures that wouldn't say boo to a goose.

This is a fairly simple sketch, not a lot going on, but sometimes I just like toying with facial expressions. In this case I decided that the fairy should look a little androgynous, like my version of Peter Pan, for no particular reason other than to explore possibilities. Whatever, if anything, comes from this sketch, I never get bored of creating characters out of nothing but a vague idea.

This is an example of getting carried away with a sketch – in a positive way, I believe – probably because it was one of my first serious fairy studies; at least it started out as a study, after finding some wonderful large toadstools in Bunny Wood in the spring.
Everyone knows, of course, that fairies use toadstools as seats on which to rest awhile when their wings get tired. This was the original thinking behind 'The Toadstool Fairy'.

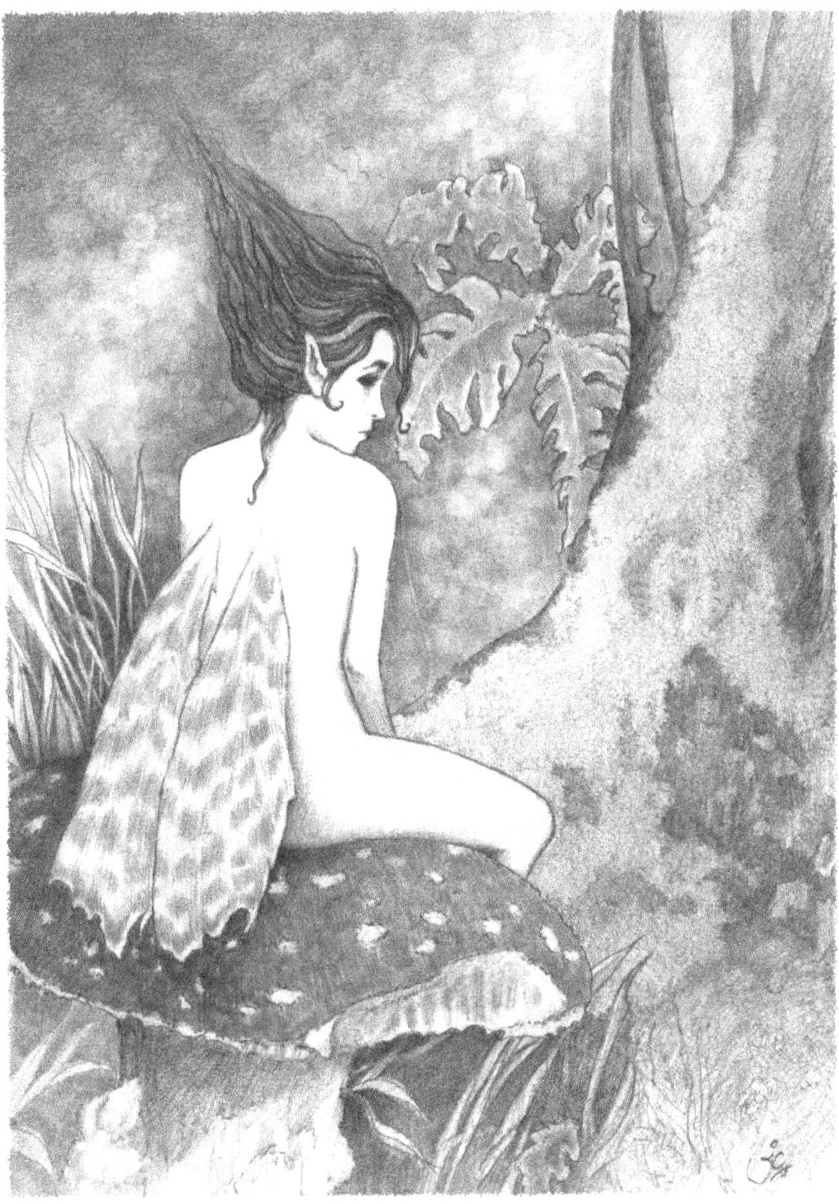

'The Toadstool Fairy'

Once I was happy with the fairy, her relaxed pose and expression and tired, drooping wings, I decided the whole sketch needed a context. One of the dark, out of the way corners of Bunny Wood that I know so well would offer her a safe place to relax, away from prying eyes.
I used a paper blender to soften the background, giving a sense of depth, together with a kneadable eraser to suggest soft, dappled light. I'm sure that, before too long, this sketch will become a full-colour illustration more or less as it looks now.

One late summer morning, close to Bunny Wood lake, I saw a solitary ripe crab apple on a small tree. This was one of those moments when you get an image in your head straight away, built around that one central object. My immediate thought was of Eve in the Garden of Eden, and how she was tempted by the serpent to eat the apple.

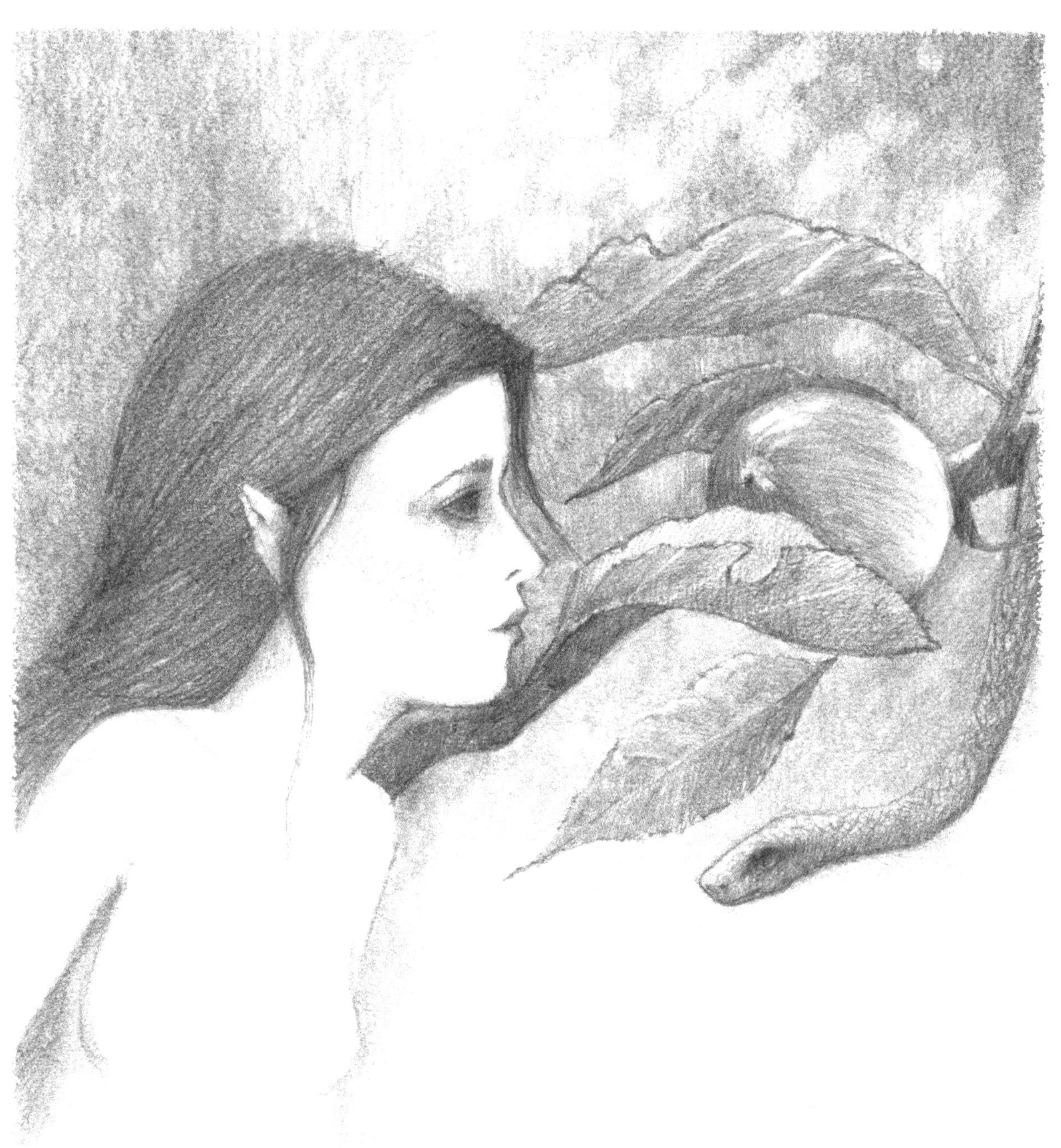

'Temptation'

As I wanted to get the idea down on paper quickly, I didn't put too much detail in the sketch. All I needed for future reference were the principal subjects – the apple, Eve and the snake – and a rough idea of the composition. Fleshing out of the final illustration, in which Eve will no doubt be replaced by a fairy, can wait until I revisit the subject. If there are any snake experts out there, try not to be too critical, I just made it up!

One morning, after some rain the night before, I came across a small water-filled tree stump in Bunny Wood. Naturally it got me wondering if it had a purpose. The answer was obvious I suppose - a fairy bath. Fairies, like us, need somewhere to bathe and wash their hair, and it occurred to me that Mother Nature is very adept at providing for the needs of all her woodland creatures.

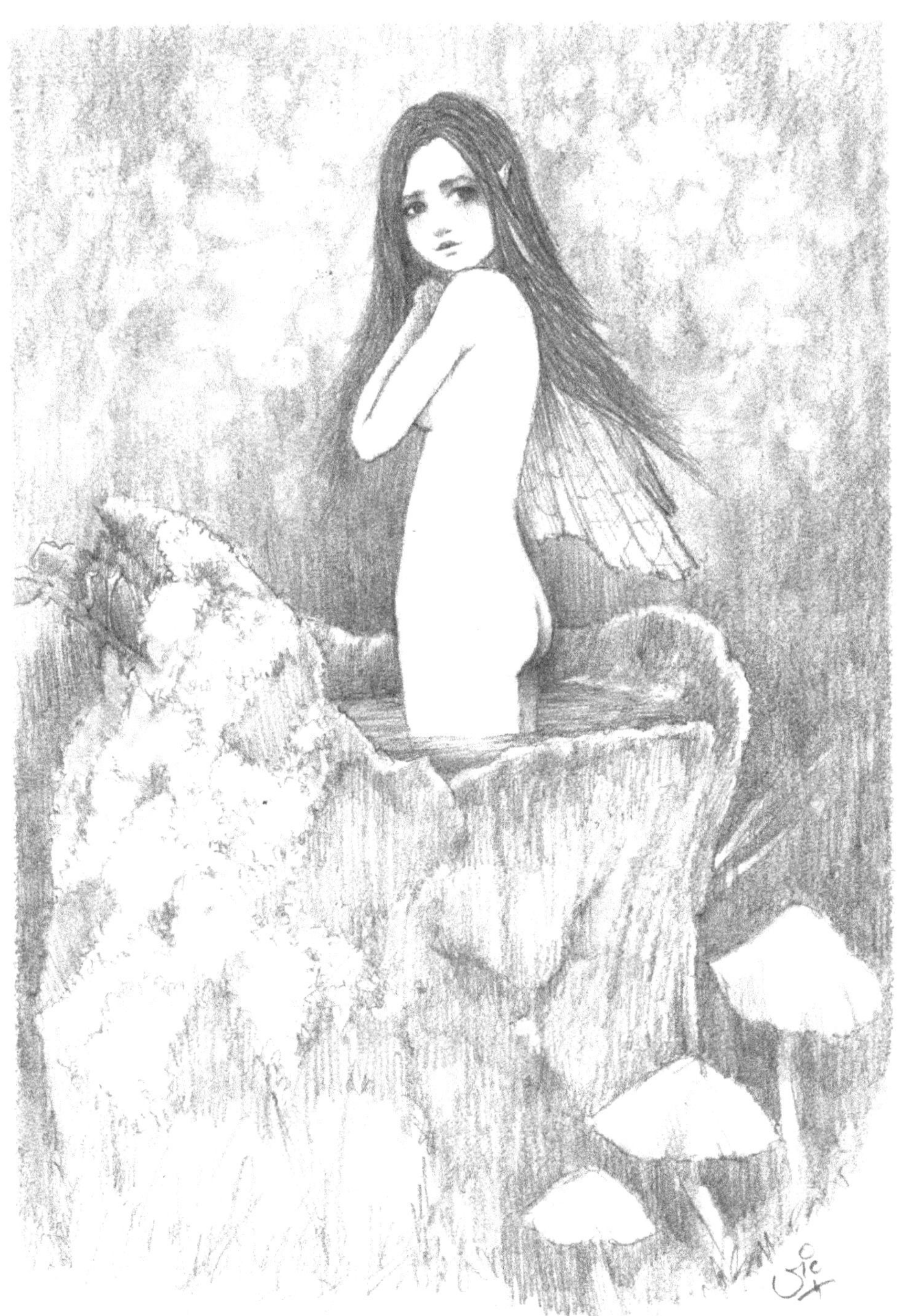

'Don't Get Your Wings Wet!'

The important elements I wanted to concentrate on in this sketch were the tree stump bath and a simple pose for the fairy; perhaps she is aware of something nearby, and so attempts to cover her modesty. This is typical of the kind of sketching I love to do; something not necessarily complete but tells, or has the making of, a story.

I love to walk around the lake when the berries and brambles are ripening. I think this is probably the time of year that the woodland creatures are happiest, with an abundance of wonderful things to eat.
I imagine that the fairies love the berry season as much as rabbits and squirrels, and one evening I started to wonder what a fairy who loves brambles might look like. An image came to mind of a child gazing longingly in a sweet shop window and all of the yummy things inside.

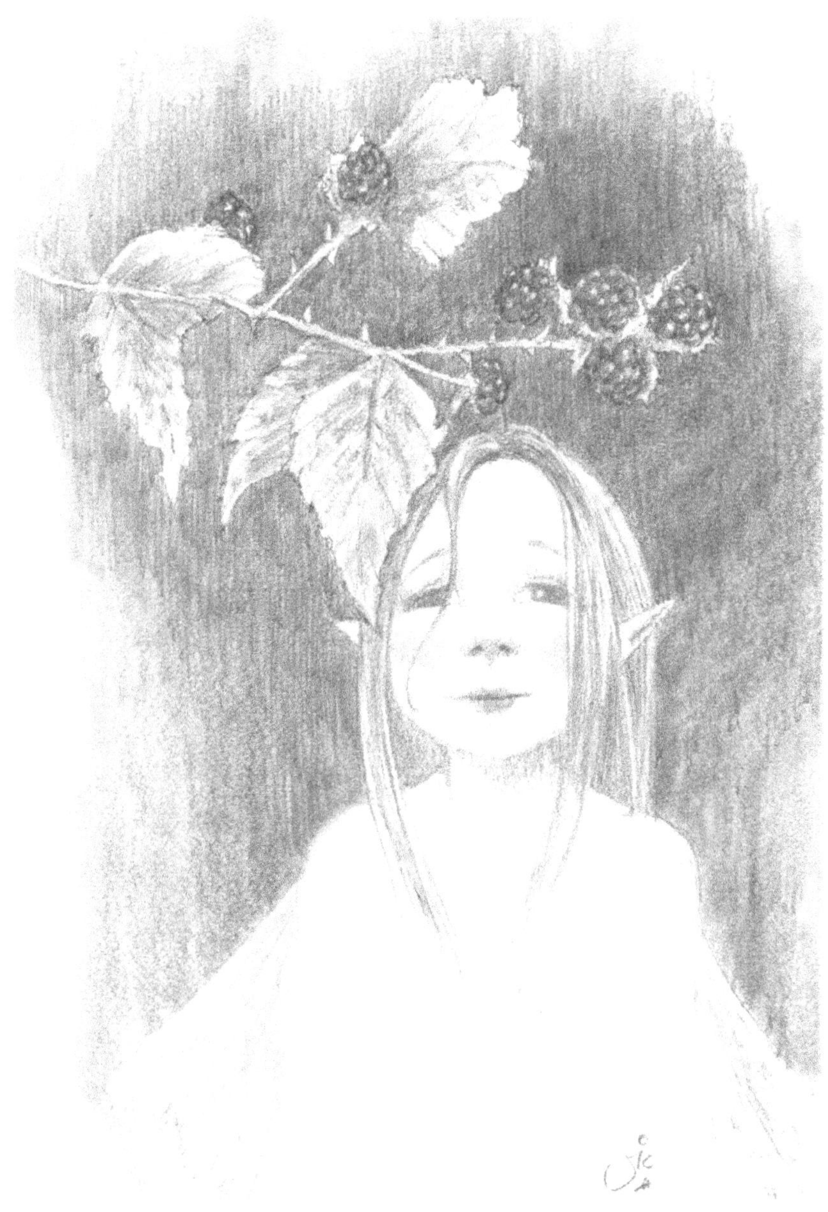

'The Bramble Fairy'

This was the expression I wanted for my bramble fairy and, after a couple of quick doodles, was happy with the resulting look. Then of course, eating brambles might stain her lips with the juice, so I gave her fuller, darker lips, rosy cheeks and hint of a red nose to match.
Finally, her eyes would have to be like dark berries with that little shiny reflection to match the fruit. For me this was a really useful couple of hours sketching, as it helped to guide me through the thought processes of creating a character with a purpose.

I love the idea of subjects interacting in an illustration, often this is an essential part of the story-telling.
I have done a few sketches now of fairies, and the like, interacting with other creatures, such as moths, squirrels, etc. This very loose sketch marks the beginning of an adventure that the fairy and the young crow, somehow bound together, are about to embark on.
What I really wanted to show, apart from what the characters might look like, was the connection between the two of them. Their expressions, full of anticipation, hopefully create an insight of the story to follow.

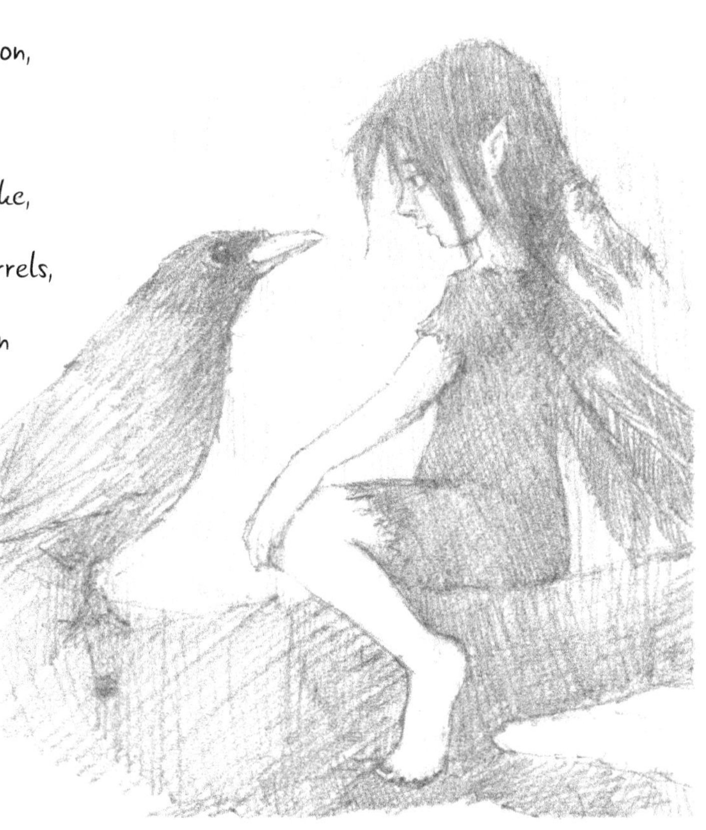

'The Crow Fairy #1'

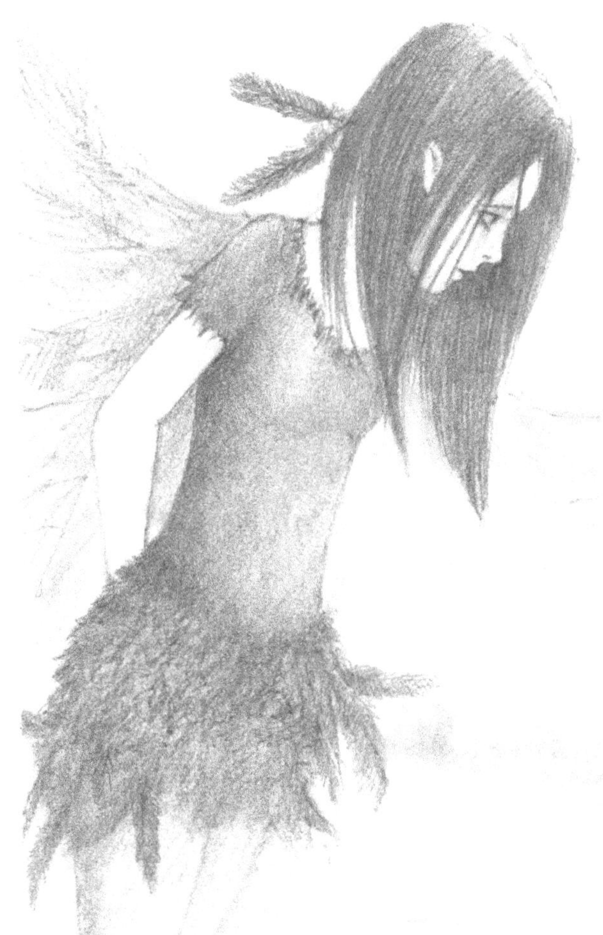

'The Crow Fairy #2'

Soon after I had sketched crow fairy #1, I wanted to see what she might look like a little more grown up, as I did previously with Red Riding Hood.
The thinking behind this sketch was partly character development, but I think mainly it was curiosity on my part. How would our dark fairy mature?
There is no sign of the crow in this sketch, purely because it is unfinished, as are the fairy's wings. What I wanted to show above all was a confident character, set high up and about to swoop into a valley far below without hesitation.
Having done both sketches I can begin to see the story potential in each of them much more clearly.

This sketch is the third phase of the 'Crow Fairy' series. In this one the fairy has grown into something more than a fairy, a whole new species almost.
The crow, her constant companion, but older of course, is still here. Perhaps the adventures they have are a little darker and more sinister now, but they are both strong-willed creatures and, together, they fear nothing.
'A Crow's Kiss' is a much more developed sketch than the previous two crow fairies, at least as far as the character is concerned. You may probably be able to tell that there is quite a Waterhouse/Pre-Raphaelite influence in the girl and her expression. For that I make no apologies, as that particular art genre ranks high among my favourites.
As with Red Riding Hood, I find myself fascinated with the idea of visualising these types of characters as they grow into adulthood.
I might find myself reproducing this image as a larger painting, perhaps in oils, in the Waterhouse style, whenever time permits, but for now, the idea of 'The Crow's Kiss' is safely stored for future use.

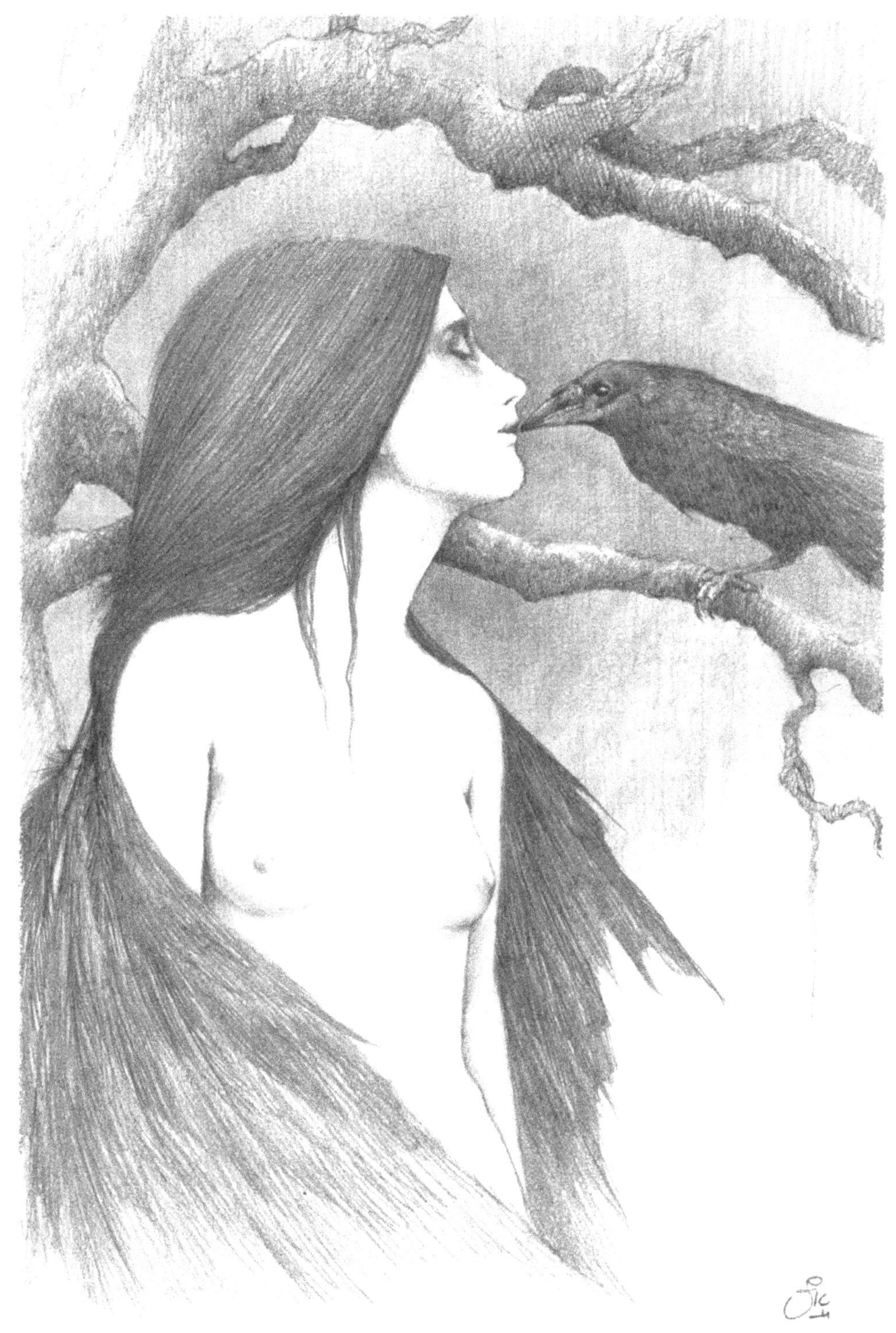

'A Crow's Kiss'

What began as a ten minute lunchtime doodle ended up surprising me as it progressed.
With no idea of where it was heading, I doodled a head of hair, followed by a simple body shape with arms and legs. Then I left it there and carried on with my other work.
Later that evening, I looked back at the doodle and decided that it should become a fairy of some sort, so I added the wings and gave her a kind of rainbow-striped dress.
The little fairy looked liked she might be pulling something behind her, so I gave her a toy rabbit on wheels.
As it needed some other elements of interest, I put her in a woodland scene with a toadstool and a tree, complete with a bird and a squirrel.
But what could the little fairy be looking at, I wondered. It had to be something small of course, so I sketched a mouse on top of the toadstool.
The question then was why was she looking at the mouse? After pondering for a few minutes, I decided that, in keeping with the rabbit toy, the mouse was a little clockwork mouse that had stopped right on top of the toadstool; hence the title.
This all goes to show that out of a ten minute doodle, a whole story can evolve.

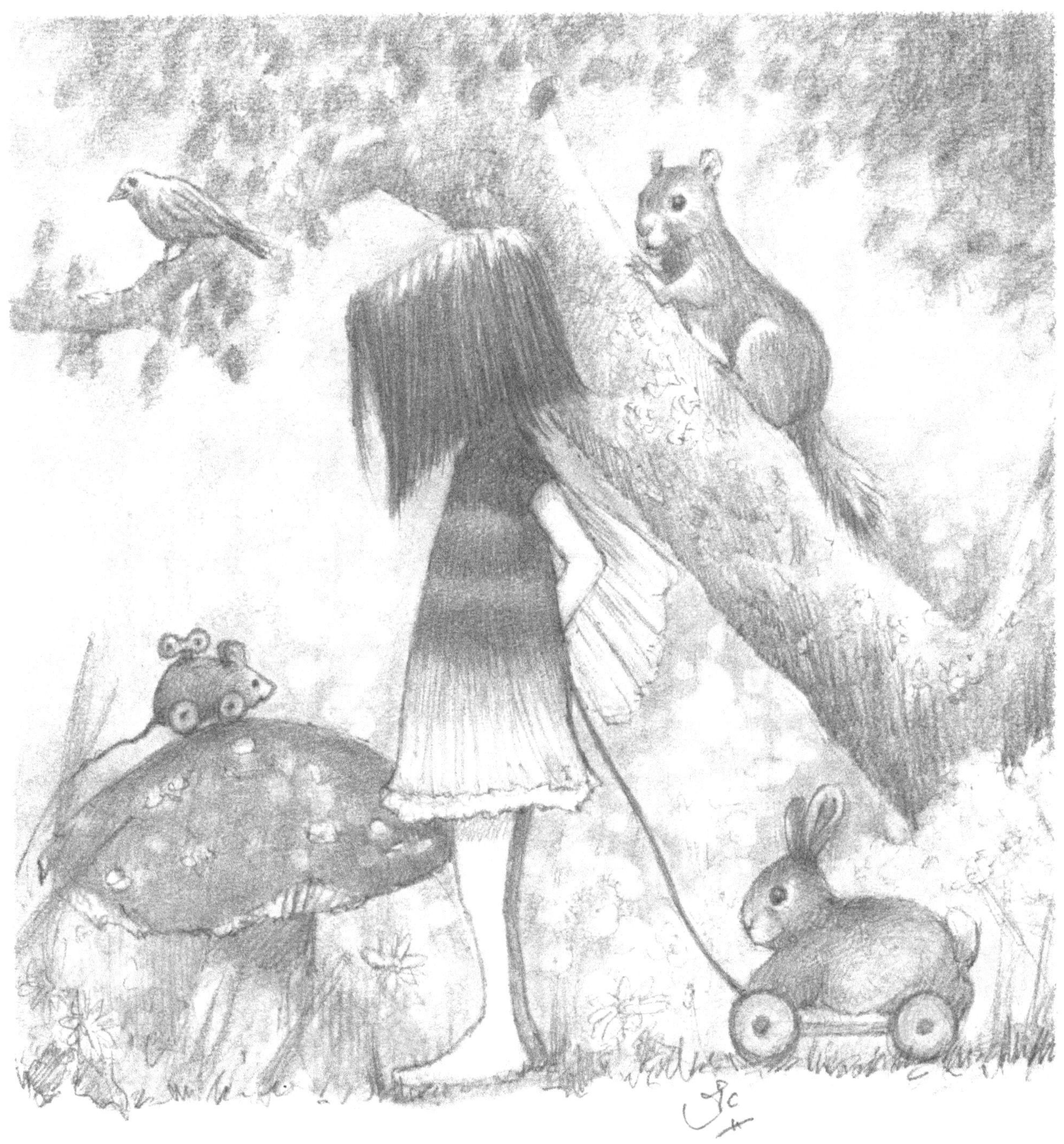

'The Mouse Ran Down'

Bearing in mind that most of the time sketching is about visualising ideas, often for future use, the end result doesn't have to be finished in the sense of it being a complete illustration.

In the case of this sketch, the idea of a bad fairy stealing acorns from squirrels as they plucked them from the tree and dropped them to the ground, came to me when I saw a squirrel doing just that one morning close to Bunny Wood.

As usual, that evening, I needed to get the idea down on paper the quickest way I know how. After about an hour the character for 'The Acorn Thief' was born.

As you can see, it is a long way from being a full illustration, but I now have a permanent reminder of what the character looks like for when I have more time to work on the story.

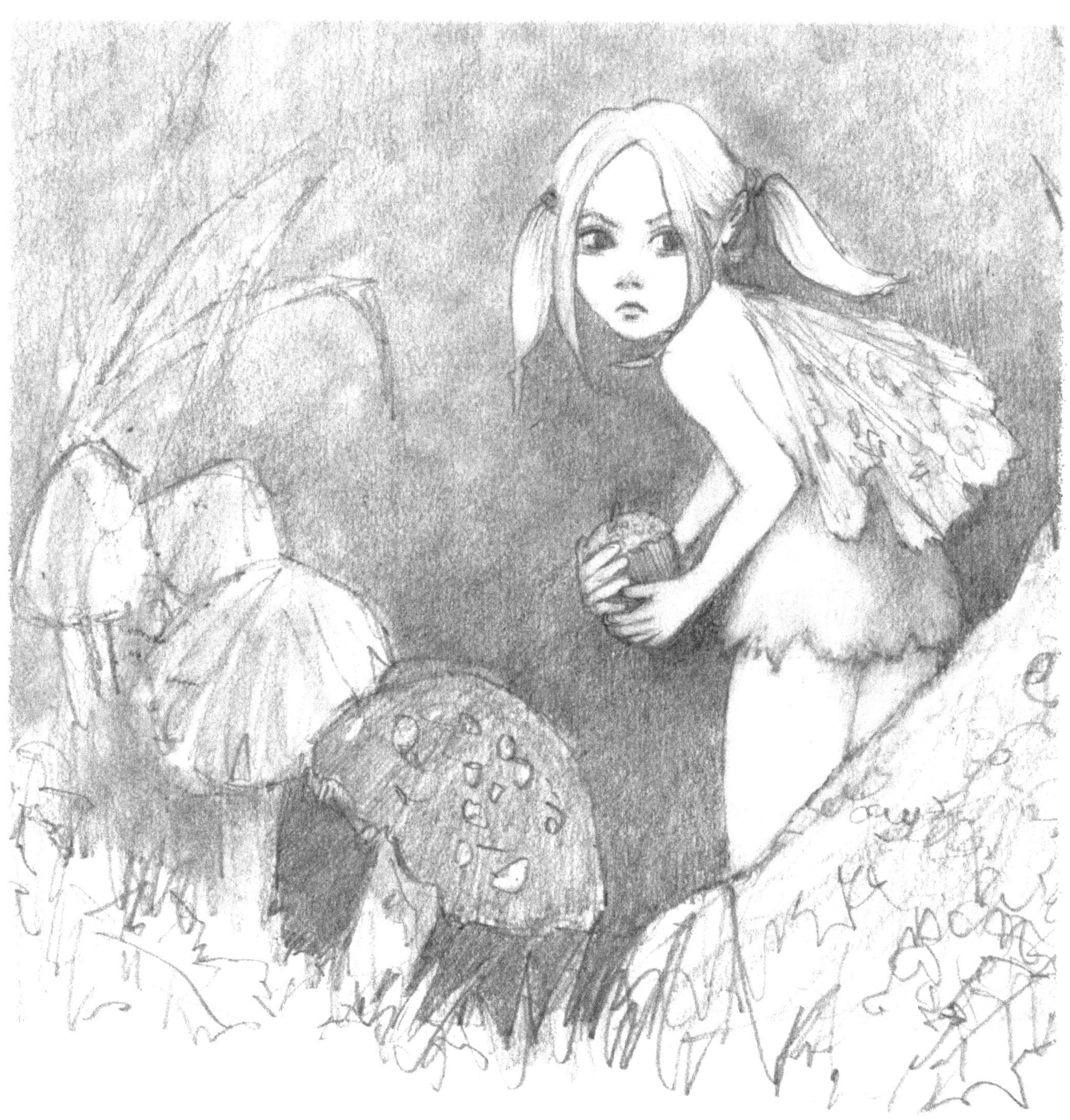

'The Acorn Thief'

After sketching the naiad, or water nymph, from J W Waterhouse's painting of the same name, I began to wonder what such a creature might look like once the Pre-Raphaelite ideal veneer was stripped away.
I imagine that, inhabiting lakes, streams and rivers, a naiad might have scaly skin in some areas. So, in all three sketches I hinted at such scales around the eyes.
Naiads often had a reputation for jealousy; Salmacis fused her body with Hermaphroditus to prevent him leaving her, for example. To suggest the more sinister side of naiads, I gave them all dark, blacked out eyes, which also hints at an 'other worldly' look.

In my first sketch, I hinted at fins on the naiad's shoulders, later rejecting that idea as it would seem more befitting a mermaid.

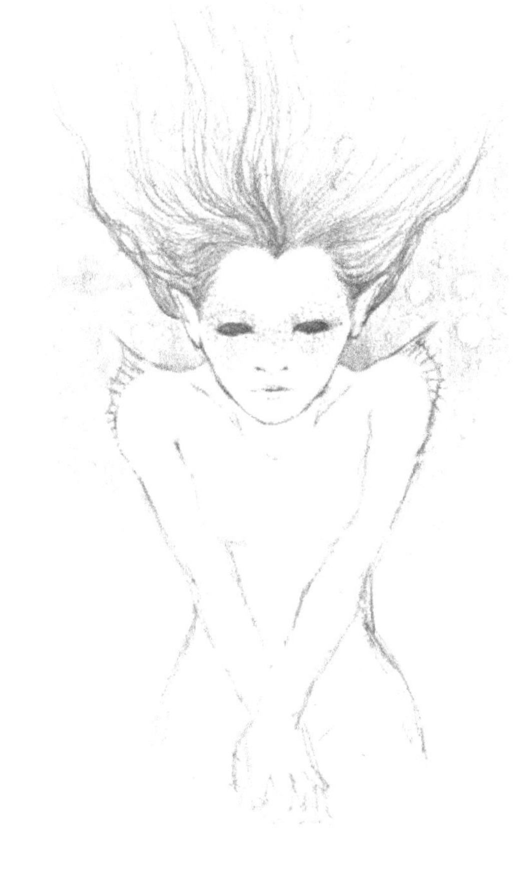

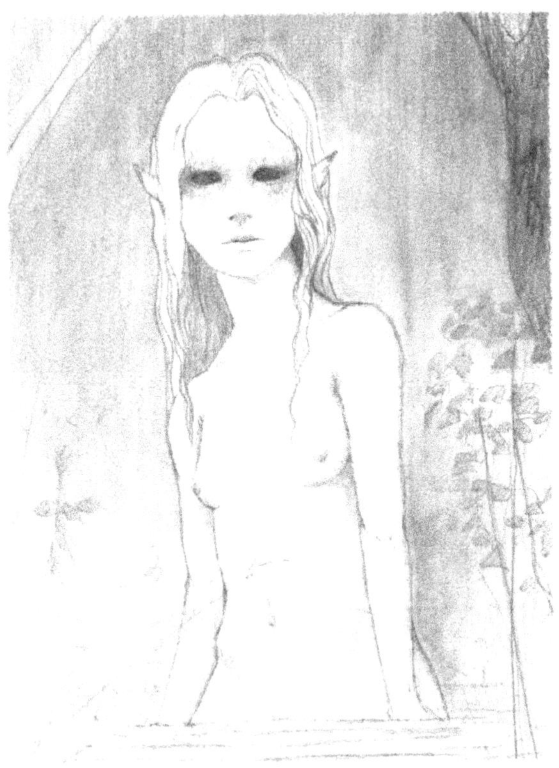

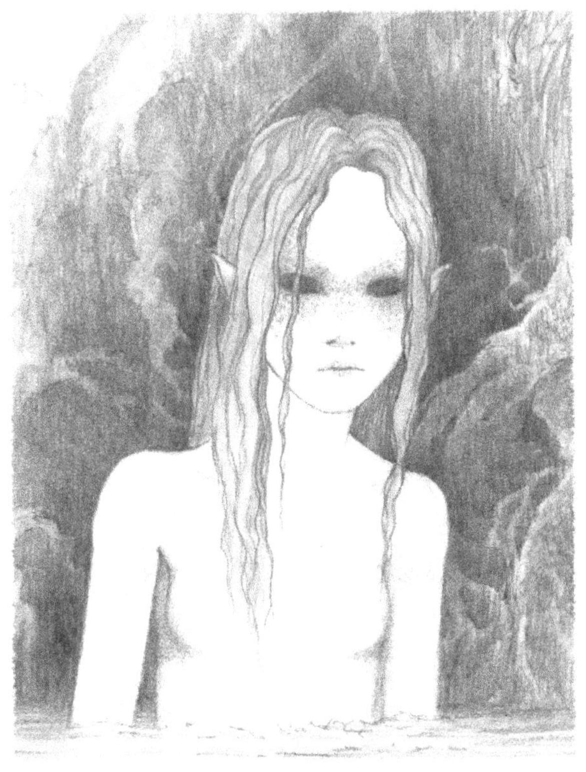

The subsequent pair of sketches fit the bill as far as I was concerned. In both cases the naiads are emerging from a dark spot at the side of a lake or river. Their hair is constantly damp and bedraggled of course and, naturally, they have no need of clothing which would be rather cumbersome when wet.
I don't know whether my naiads will ever feature in future illustrations, paintings or stories but, just in case, at least I now understand them a little more.

There are certain times of the year that suggest what to sketch on an evening.
Halloween, of course, conjures up all kinds of images. For me, at a time when a lot of my sketches were story-book characters, fairies and trolls, I decided to try my hand at a witch.
This witch, as you can see, has taken on some of the facial attributes of my fairy sketches; on the outside not too wicked, but if you were to push her...

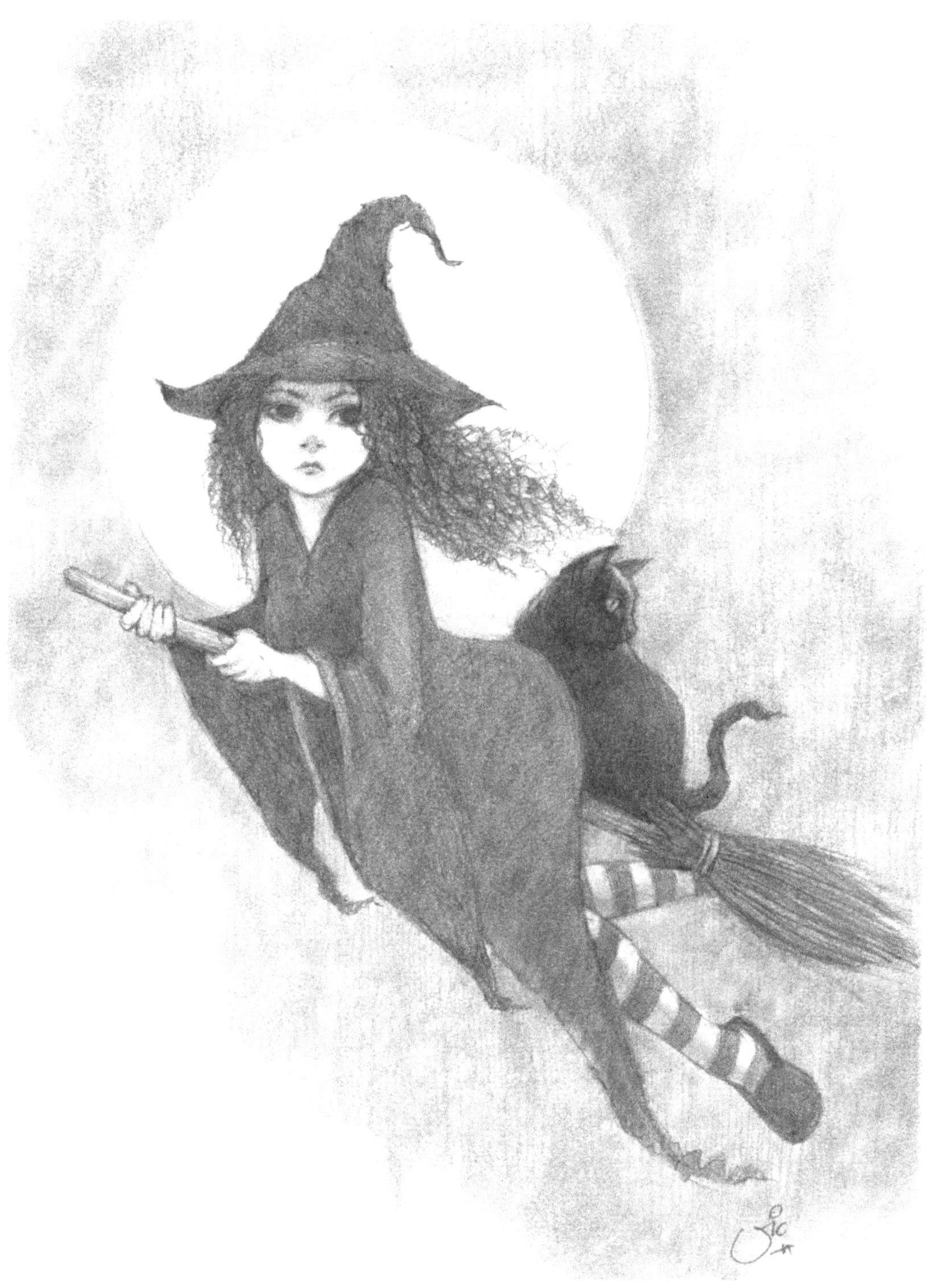

'Fly Me to the Moon'

The witch's familiar was easy to find. Marley, one of our black cats, fit the bill perfectly, especially as he has just the right attitude. The full moon in the background was an afterthought, just something to fill out the sketch, but, once it was there, the title jumped right out at me!

After I sketched 'Fly me to the Moon', I wanted to do a more complete Halloween illustration, as Liz thought we could use the prints for raising funds for cat welfare.

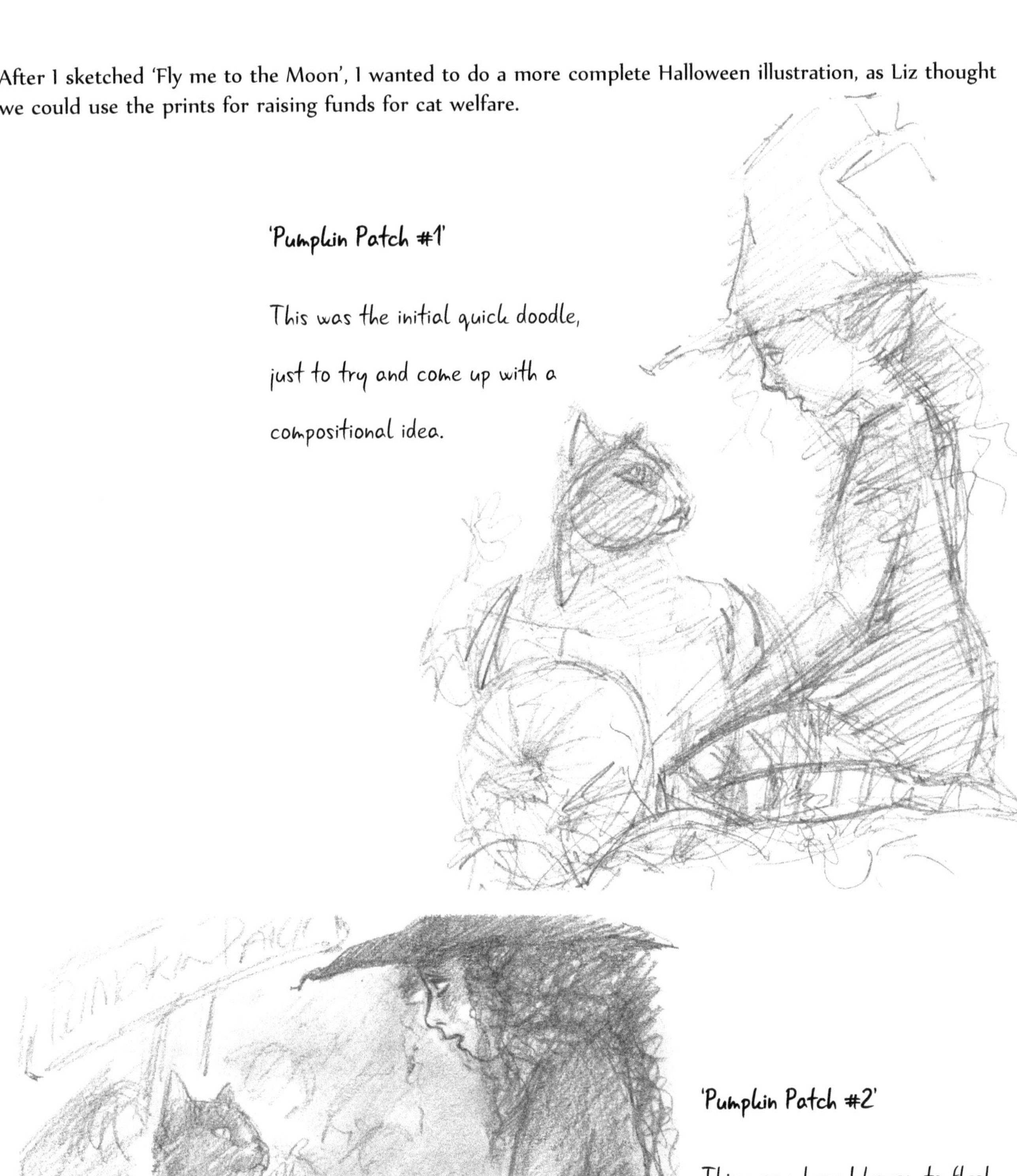

'Pumpkin Patch #1'

This was the initial quick doodle, just to try and come up with a compositional idea.

'Pumpkin Patch #2'

This was where I began to flesh out the characters and details in a loose sketch format.

Both the initial doodle and loose sketch were invaluable in the creation of the final 'Pumpkin Patch' illustration, which features Marley the cat and Rodney the rook.

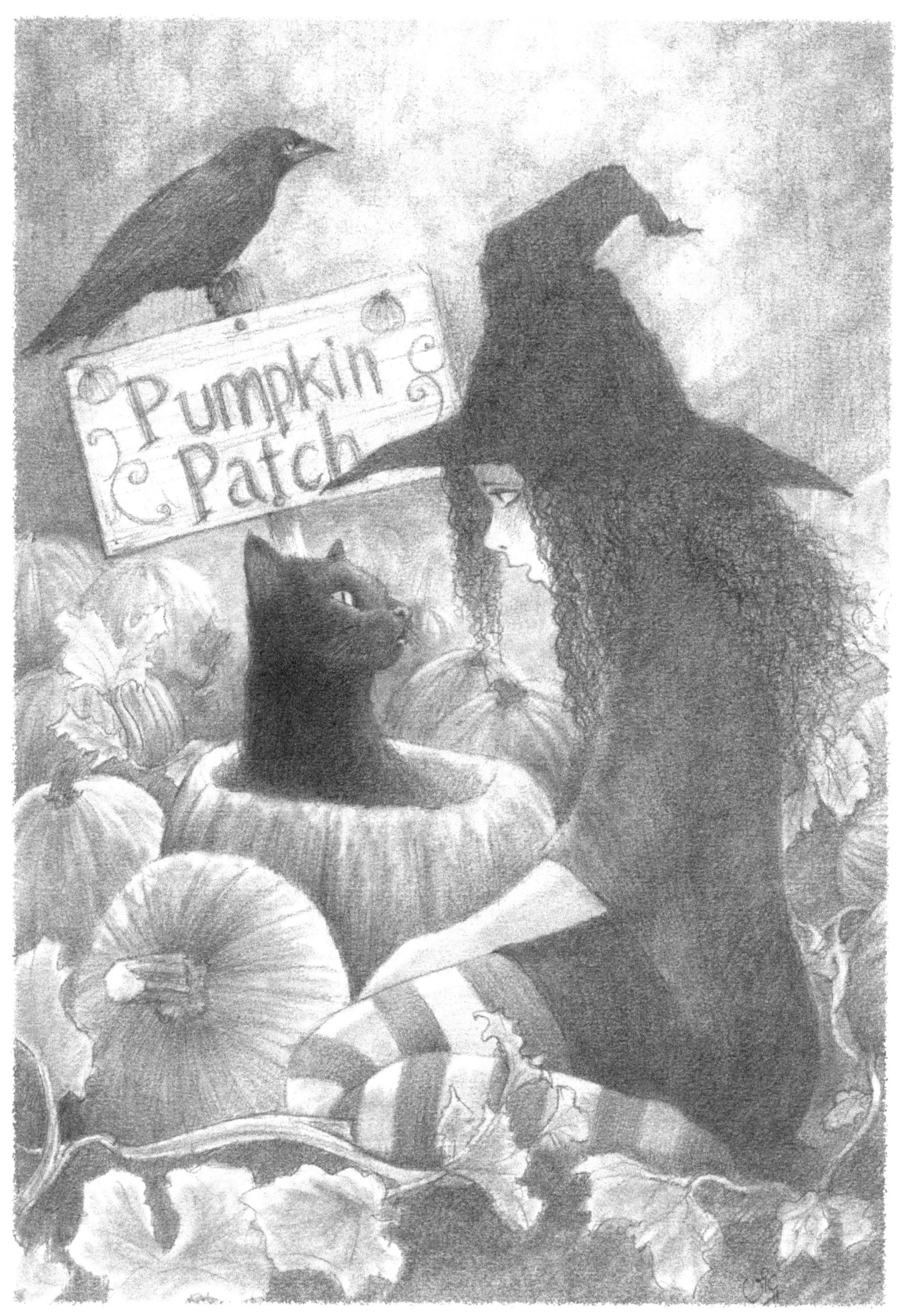

'The Pumpkin Patch'

Bits and Pieces

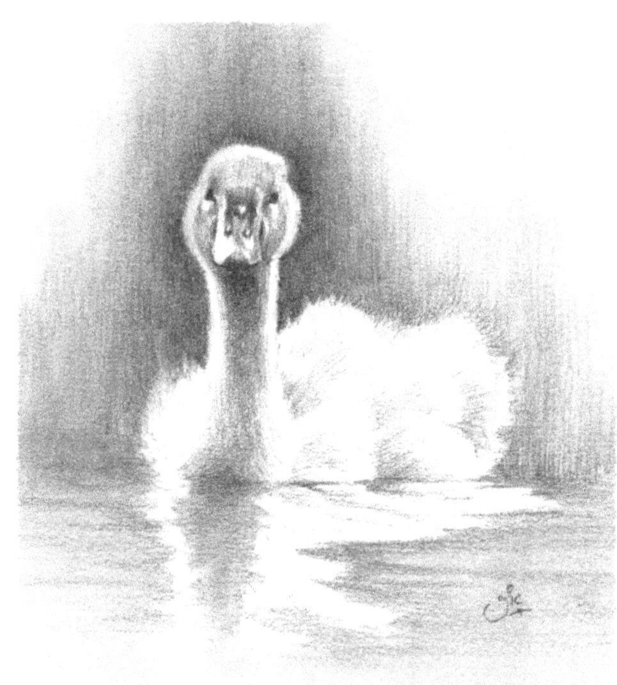

'Swanlet'

This year, on Bunny Wood lake, we were blessed with five cygnets, and it has been wonderful watching them all grow up throughout the year. I loved seeing them in the early mornings, when they first took to the water, and the sun was low, giving them an almost halo – lighting effect. This sketch was made as a reminder of those special moments; perhaps leading to a more complete illustration or painting at some point.

'Mr Bumble'

Bees, like too much of our wildlife, are under threat. It was a real pleasure, therefore, to see a number of wild bees around Bunny Wood and the surrounding fields throughout the summer. As of yet, there are still plenty of wildflowers and 'weeds' for them to feed on.

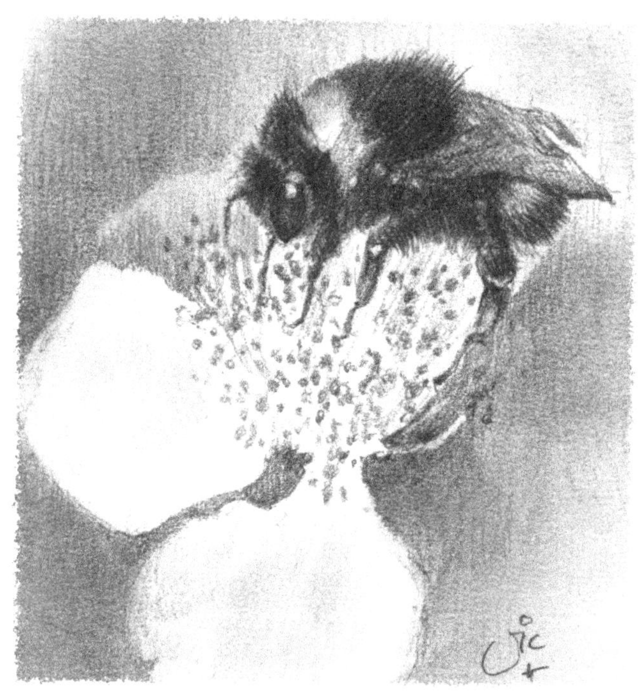

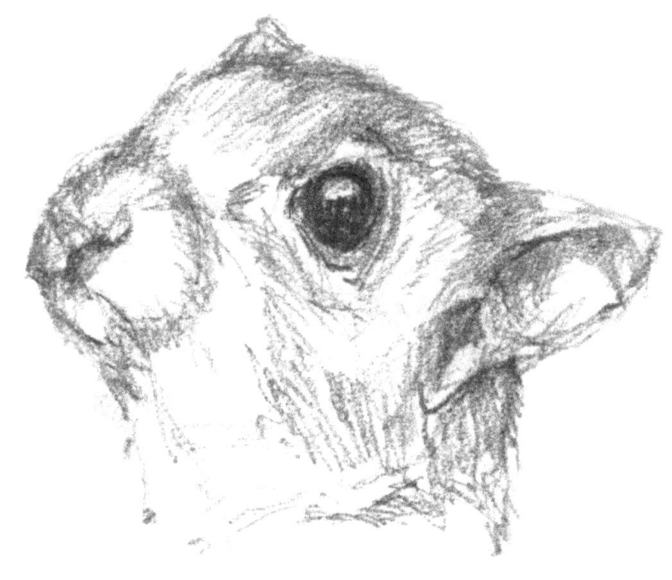

'Surprised Squirrel'

The squirrels of Bunny Wood can be difficult to photograph sometimes, especially when I'm walking the dogs, as they naturally tend to be wary of them. This quick doodle was inspired by the look I saw on one of the squirrels' faces as he/she was caught by surprise, close to the ground one morning and quickly sought shelter on a higher tree branch.

FEATHERED FRIENDS

In addition to the swans that nest on Bunny Wood lake each year, there is an abundance of waterfowl and other birds; so many that I haven't got round to sketching them all yet, so here are just a few that made their way into my sketchbook from the comfort of the sofa.

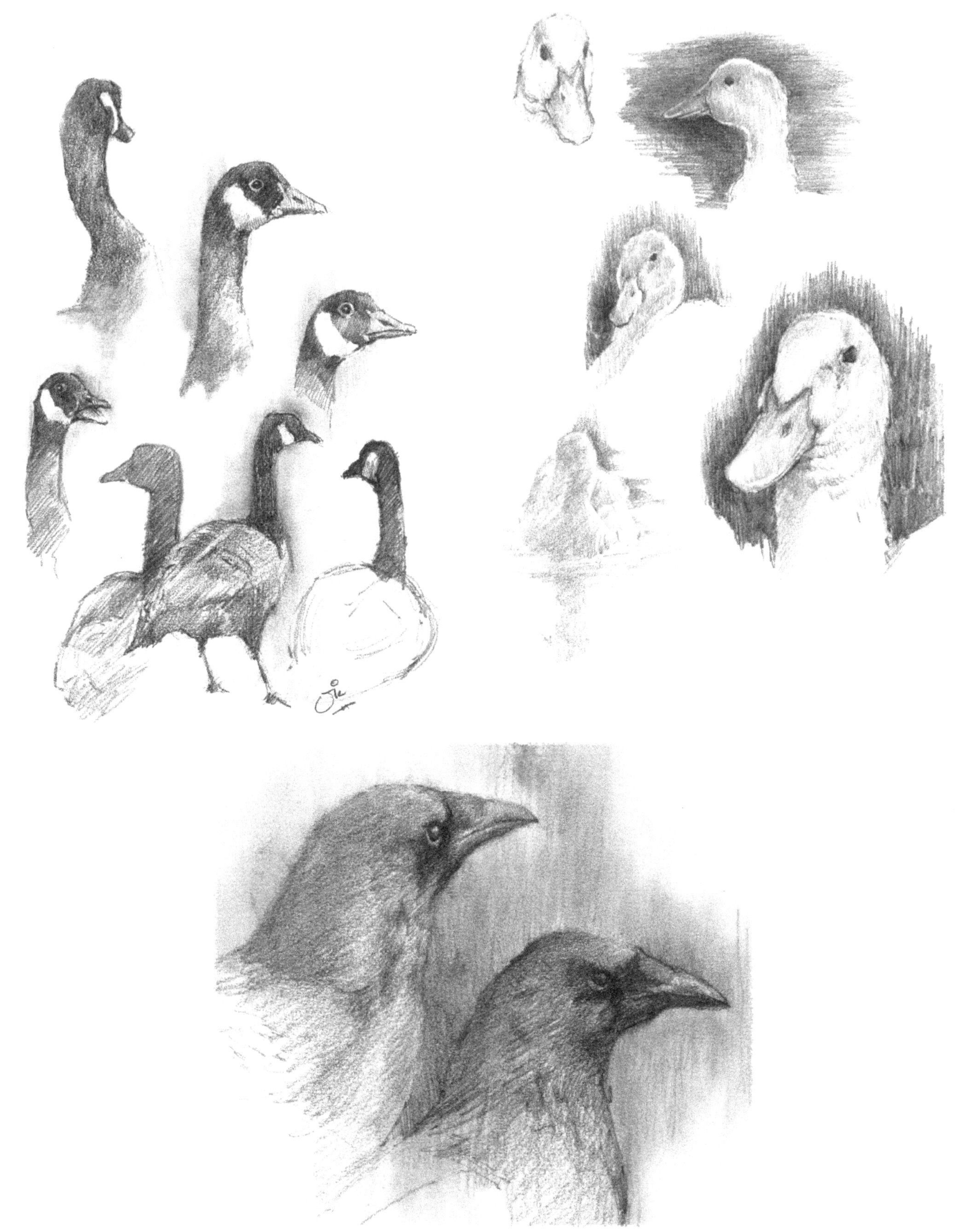

'Ducks, Canada Geese & Crows'

A TALE OF TWO OTTERS

This is a pre-illustration sketch for another animal short story. One day, when we were walking the dogs in the 'Big Wood', we found this watery lair. I wondered what or who might be dwelling there. Later on, a story popped into my head, which I began sketching out one evening and finished early the following morning. Looks like it could be an ideal nesting place for Mr and Mrs Otter, but is it safe?

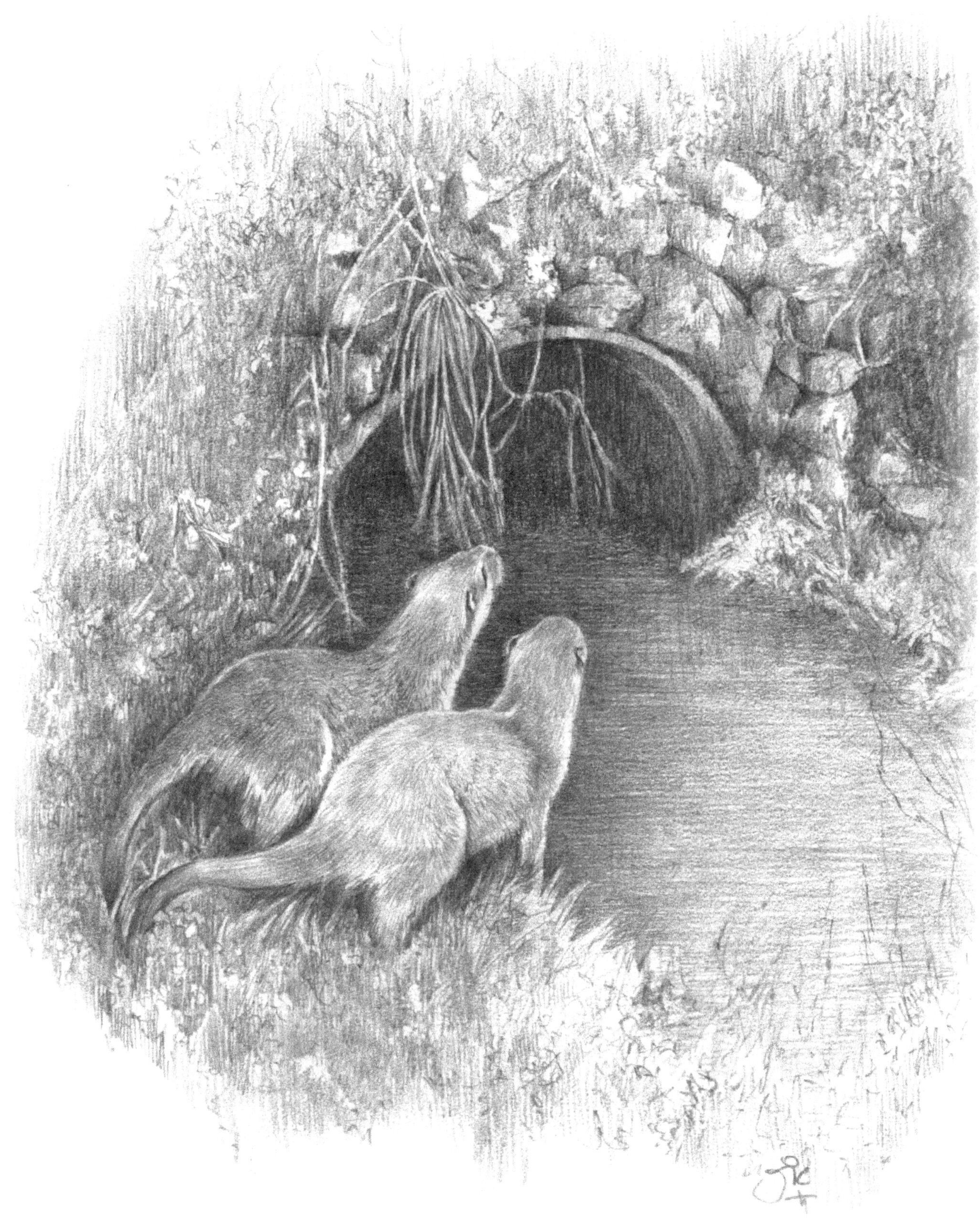

'A Tale of Two Otters'

'Ratty'

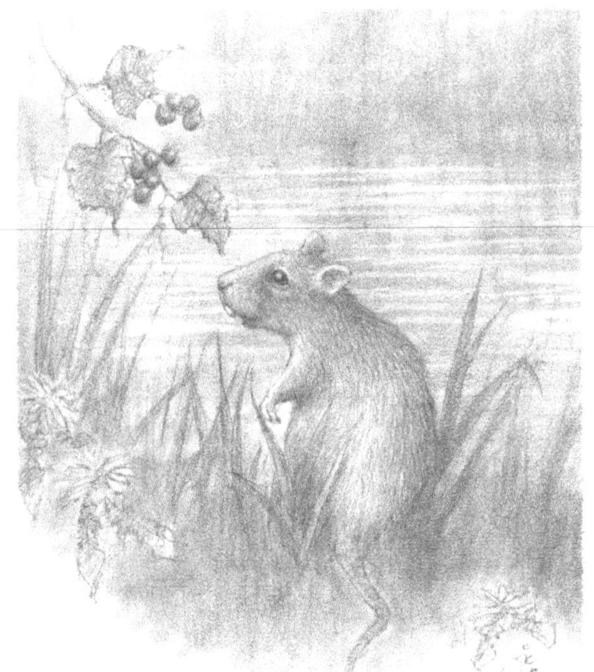

This is a character study based on a rather cute brown rat that I've seen occasionally along the water's edge at Bunny Wood. I have tried to portray the often despised rat into an amiable character that might encourage people to see them as I do; one of nature's creations just trying to get along in life.

'Chipmunk'

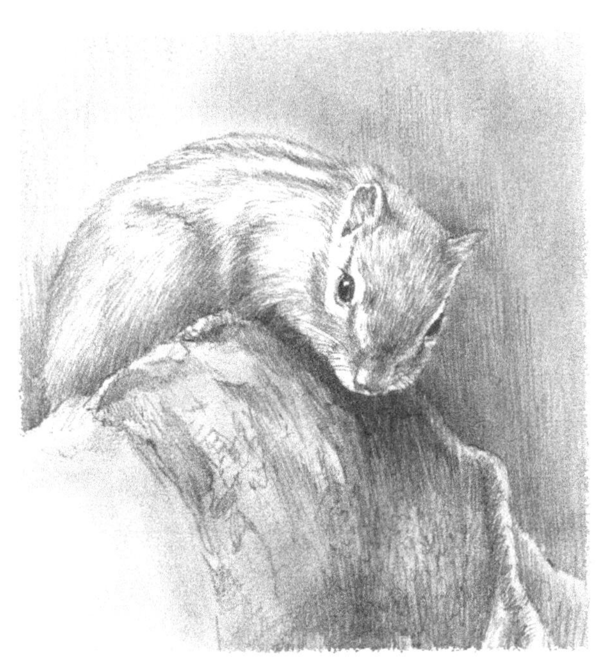

The chipmunk here was one that I spent quite a bit of time observing and photographing at Marwell Zoo a few years ago. Often in zoos the smaller creatures are passed by in favour of the larger more popular exhibits. I just loved the way this little one scurried around an old tree branch, seemingly taking as much interest in me as I did it. When I recently rediscovered my photos and made this sketch, all memories of that curious nature came back to me. Hopefully I managed to capture that in the sketch.

'Raccoon'

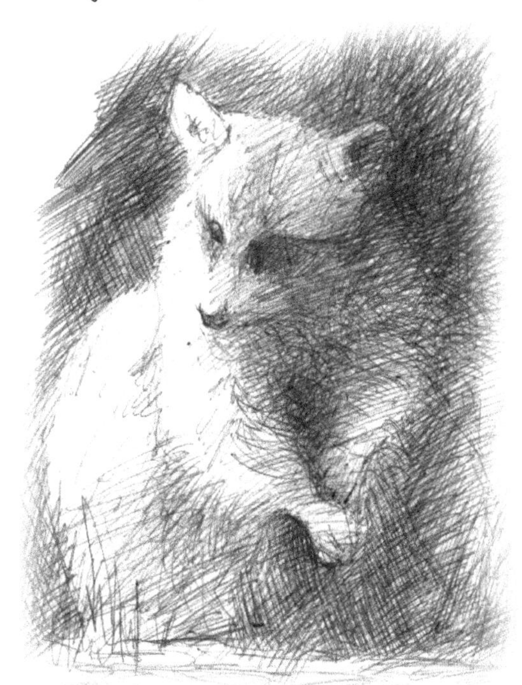

Occasionally if I want to doodle, and my pencils are somewhere else, I will use a ballpoint pen, which gives interesting results, especially as any marks made cannot be erased. Often this can produce a doodle or a sketch with a lot of energy. This raccoon, 'Bonnie', is one that we took for a walk a few years ago at the Moonridge Animal Sanctuary in California.

Sofa sketching is often a good time to explore painting possibilities. Here are two such examples; both sketched in ink in hotel rooms.

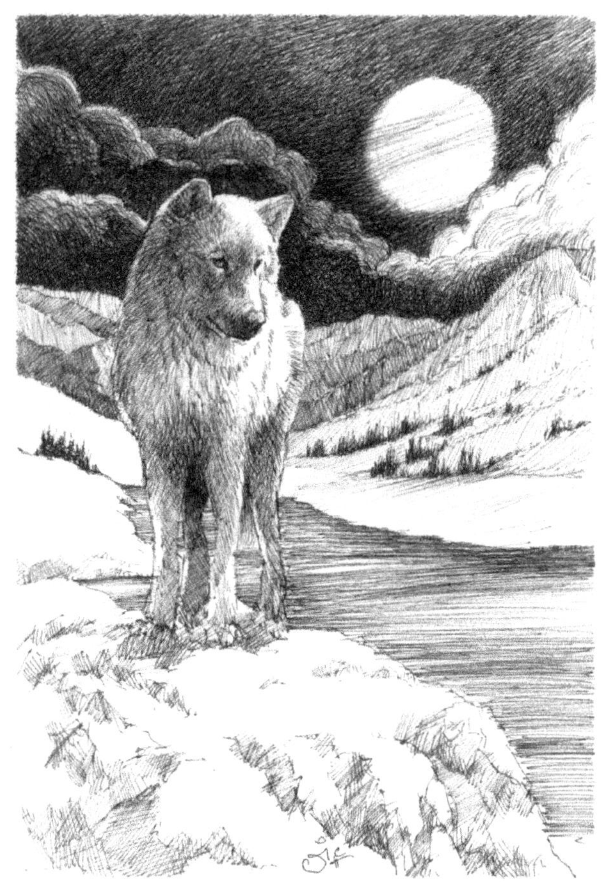

'Arctic Wolf'

The Arctic wolf was to be the subject of an upcoming pastel workshop that I was running. I had the photo reference for the wolf but, beyond that, little idea of the final image.

A quite evening's doodling with a pen created this image which provided me with the workshop painting composition.

'Bandar Log'

A couple of years ago, after I had started a series of Indian ink paintings based on Jungle Book characters, I had an idea for a follow-up painting of the 'Bandar Log', also from the Jungle Book stories. I had already taken some photographs and made some life sketches of gibbons in various poses at Marwell Zoo. One evening, while staying in a hotel during an art exhibition, I began to sketch an idea, in pen, of a possible composition for the intended painting.

This is that first compositional idea which, to date, is still on the back burner. Perhaps it will be completed in time for the next exhibition.

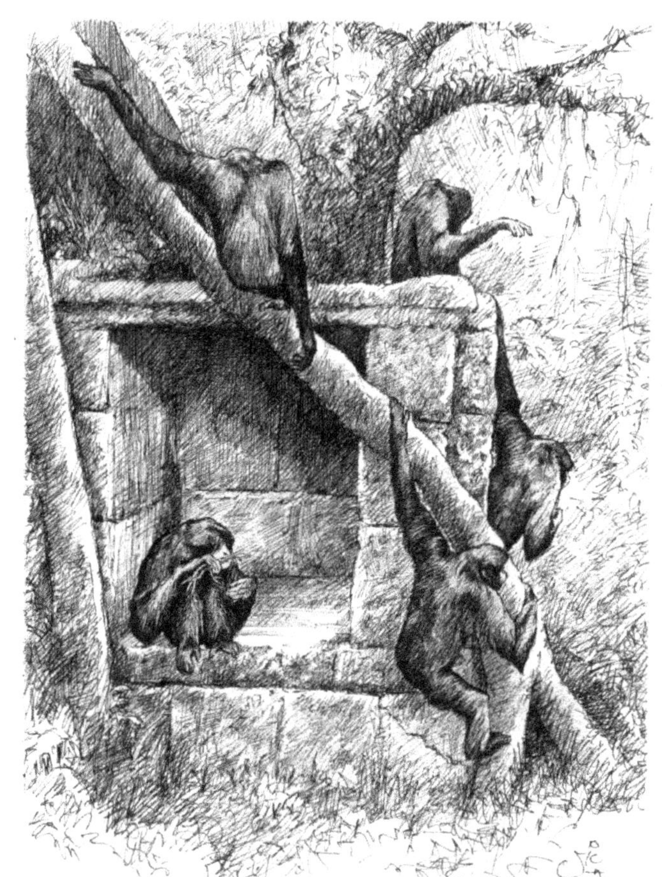

The reason for the title of this sketch will become apparent when I tell you that, a couple of Christmases ago, I gave Liz a novelty wolf head hat.
Traditionally on Christmas morning, we take the dogs for a walk in the woods, not far from home.
Liz decided to wear the wolf hat, of course, and I took some photographs. I noticed that when she lowered her head, it looked like the wolf hat had become a wolf 'head'.
This was the obvious inspiration for a fun, festive ink sketch, to which I added the church, graveyard and full moon for the final effect.

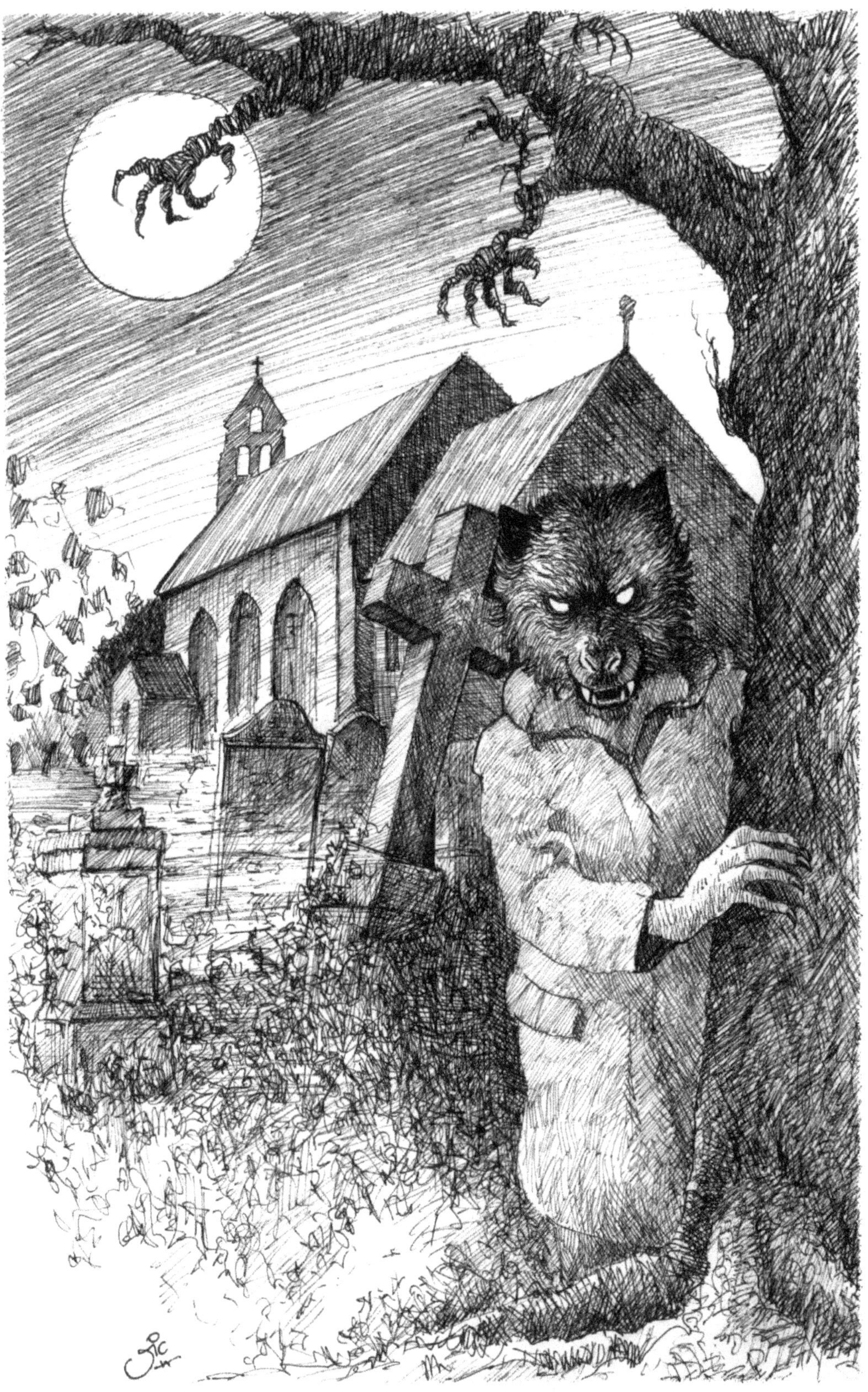

'The Christmas Werewolf'

This, as yet, unfinished sketch remains 'untitled' simply because I'm not really sure what it is.
The sketch began by trying to create an ancient Egyptian-looking character with crinkled dark hair and a headdress.
From that starting point, the rest of the sketch just seemed to grow, with bits like the 'mechanical' snakes and strange Japanese-looking hieroglyphs evolving from simple curves and lifted-out highlights.
I had originally put reflected highlights in her eyes, but soon decided that they made the 'whatever-she-is' look too human. Once I had blacked out her eyes completely she took on the appearance of an ancient deity or spirit of some kind. The creation, as it stands, is very much a work-in-progress, but one that I look forward to revisiting at some stage.

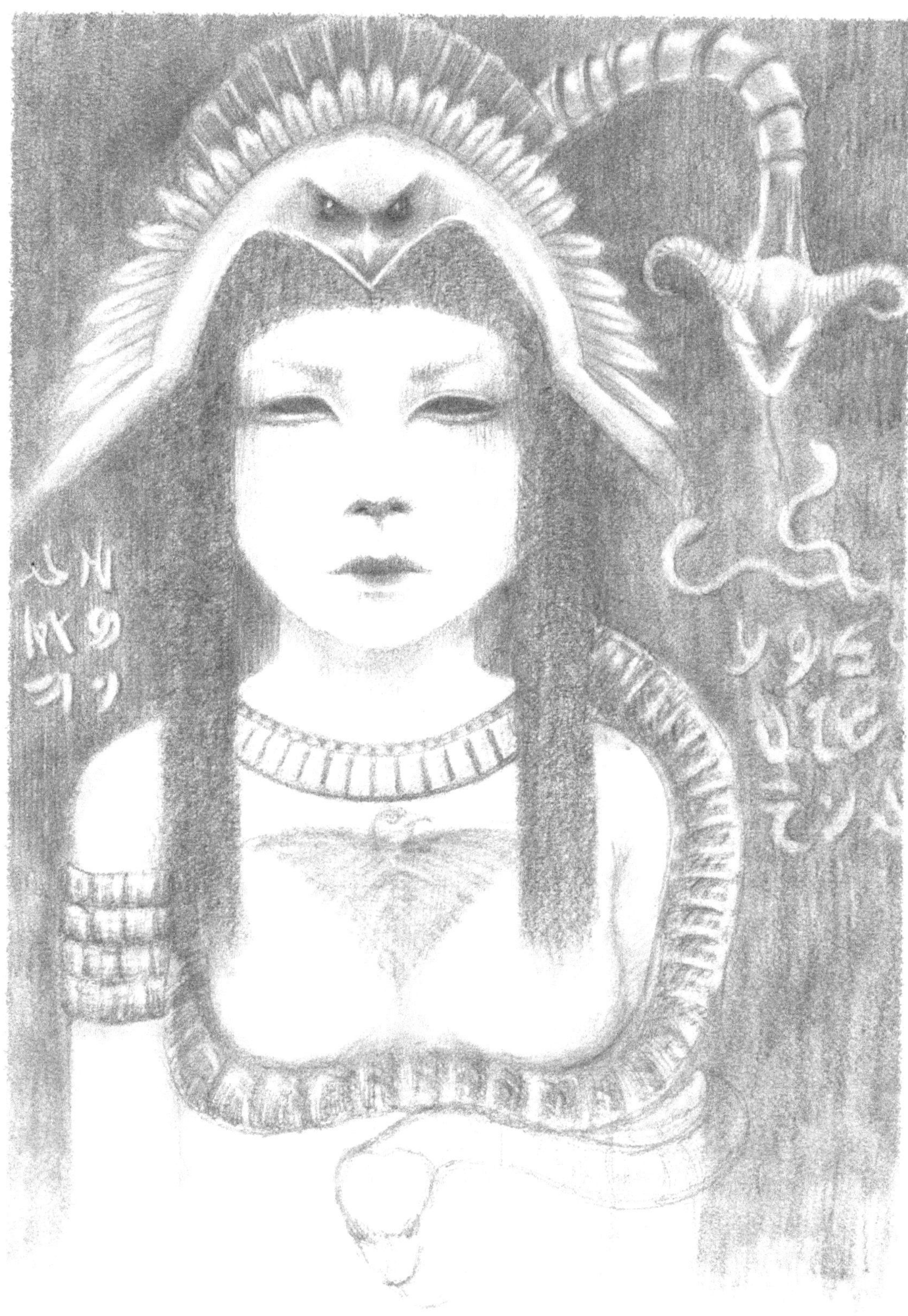

'Untitled'

CEMETERY ANGELS

These are a few of the doodles and sketches made while working on ideas for 'Dark Angels', my book of Gothic ink illustrations. Cemetery angels make great subjects for sketching, as they tend not to move too much!

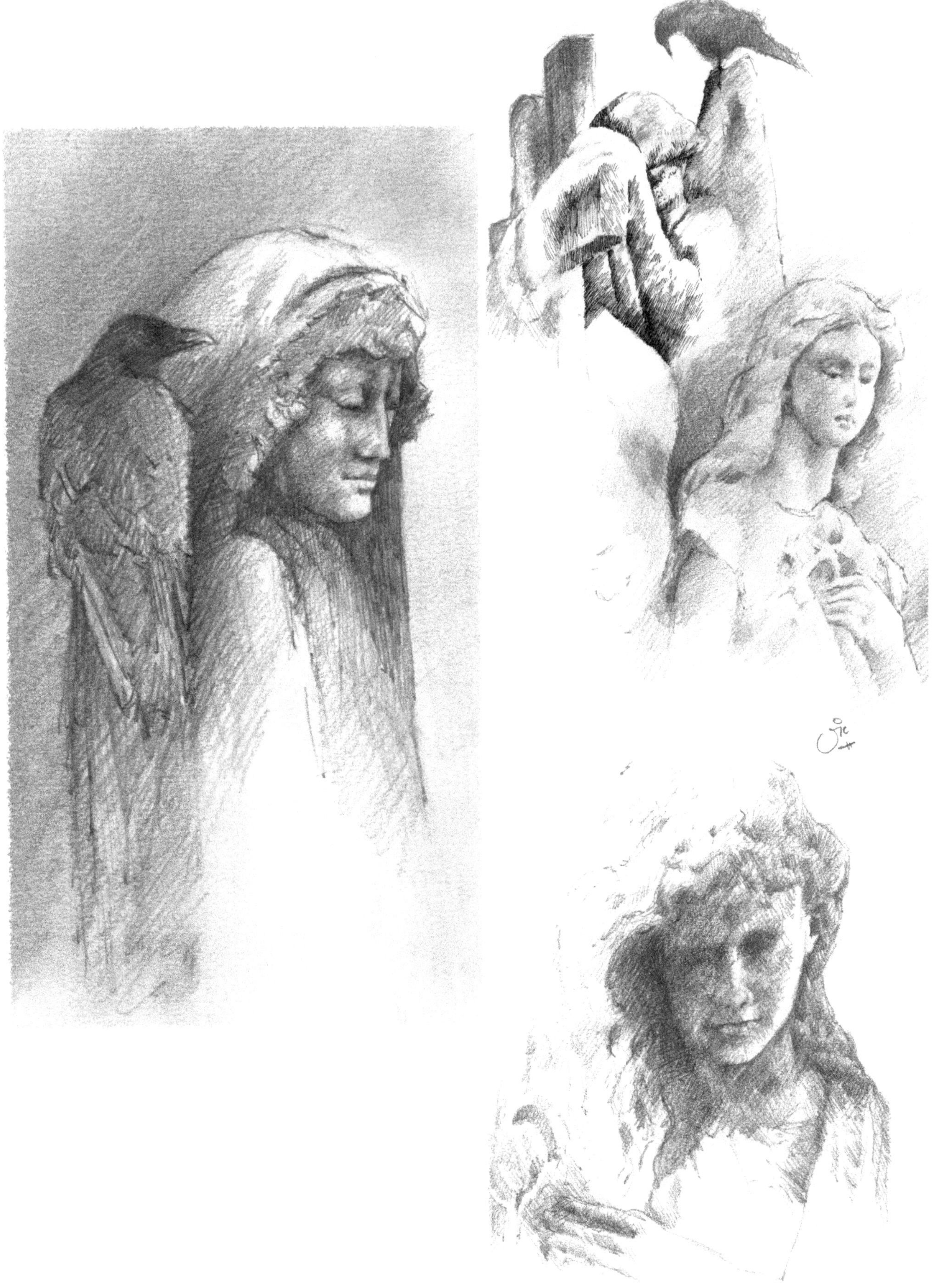

Cats

Having so many cats here (eleven at the time of writing) means there is never a shortage of feline sketching subjects. When you live with cats, they do show their individual characters and, in our home at least, create little stories around the things that they get up to.
Here are just a few of those stories in 'sofa sketch' form, some of which defy explanation, but then again is an explanation always needed?

This sketch was born out of a snapshot that my partner, Liz, took of one of our cats, Agnes. I think Liz took the photograph on our bed as Agnes was looking down. Immediately I saw it, the idea of creating a demonic cat, 'Lucy Fur', came to mind. Naturally, the setting and everything else had to be right, so I set about adding bat wings and a pointed tail. I also made the ears a little more pointed, like a devil's horns. The background is meant to represent a feline version of Hades, complete with burning fires, created with a kneadable eraser, and fish bones.

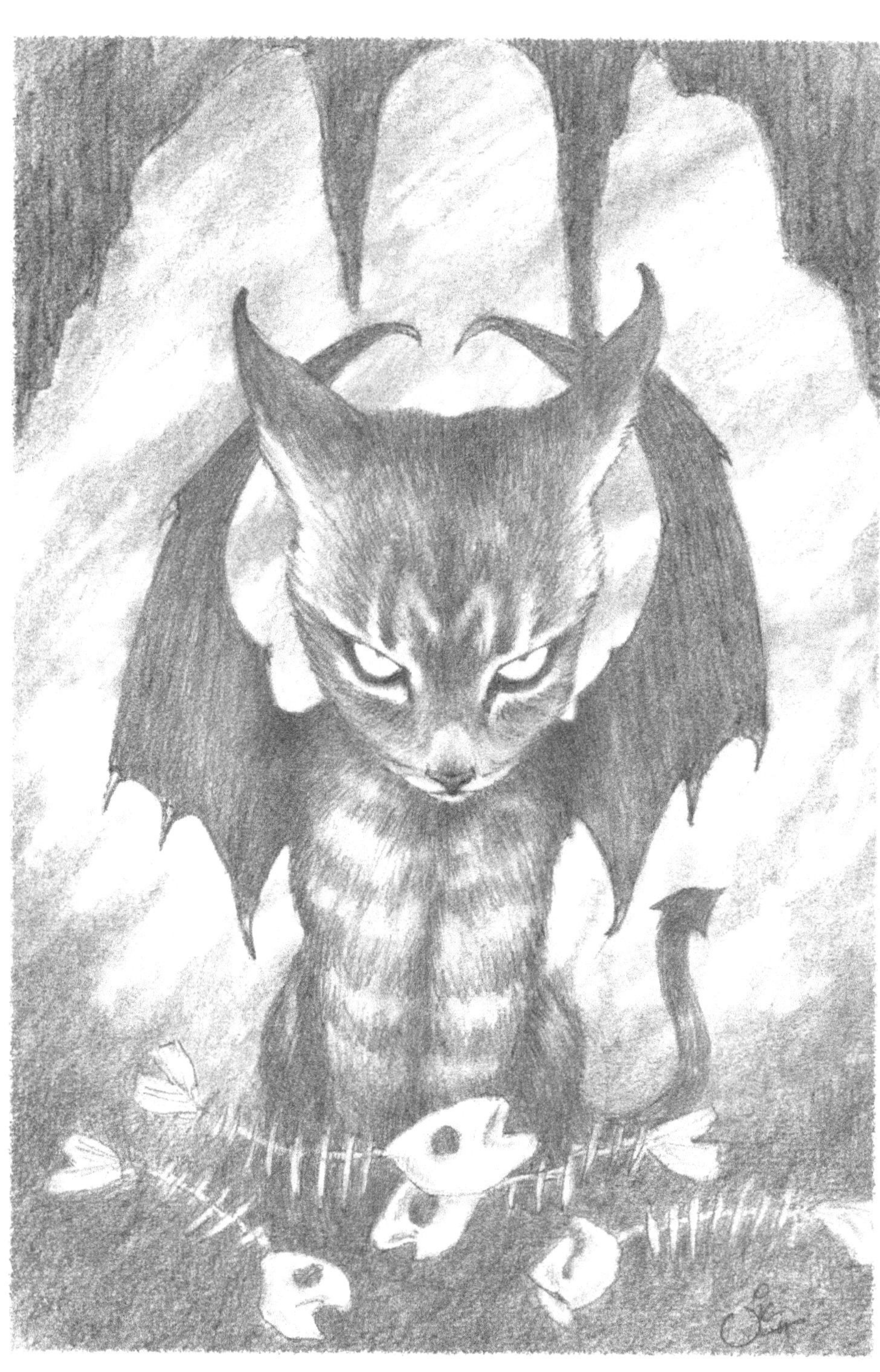

'Lucy Fur'

The final touch was to slightly exaggerate a tabby cat's 'M'-shaped marking on the forehead. In the case of 'Lucy Fur' that 'M' stands for Mephistopheles of course!

'Phoebe Kittyhawk'

'Watch in amazement as ace pilot Phoebe Kittyhawk single-handedly takes on the combined might of the notorious Flying Hellcats!'

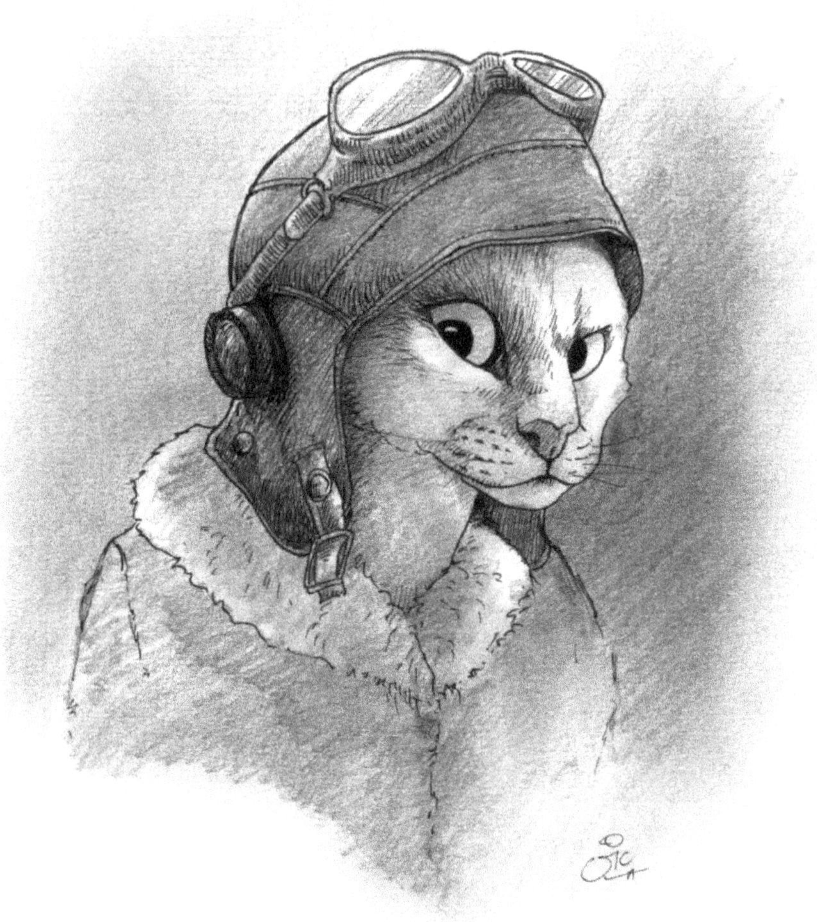

'Cross my Paw with Dreamies'

Phoebe in another role as a gipsy fortune teller, inspired by her peeking out from under a tassled sofa throw one evening.

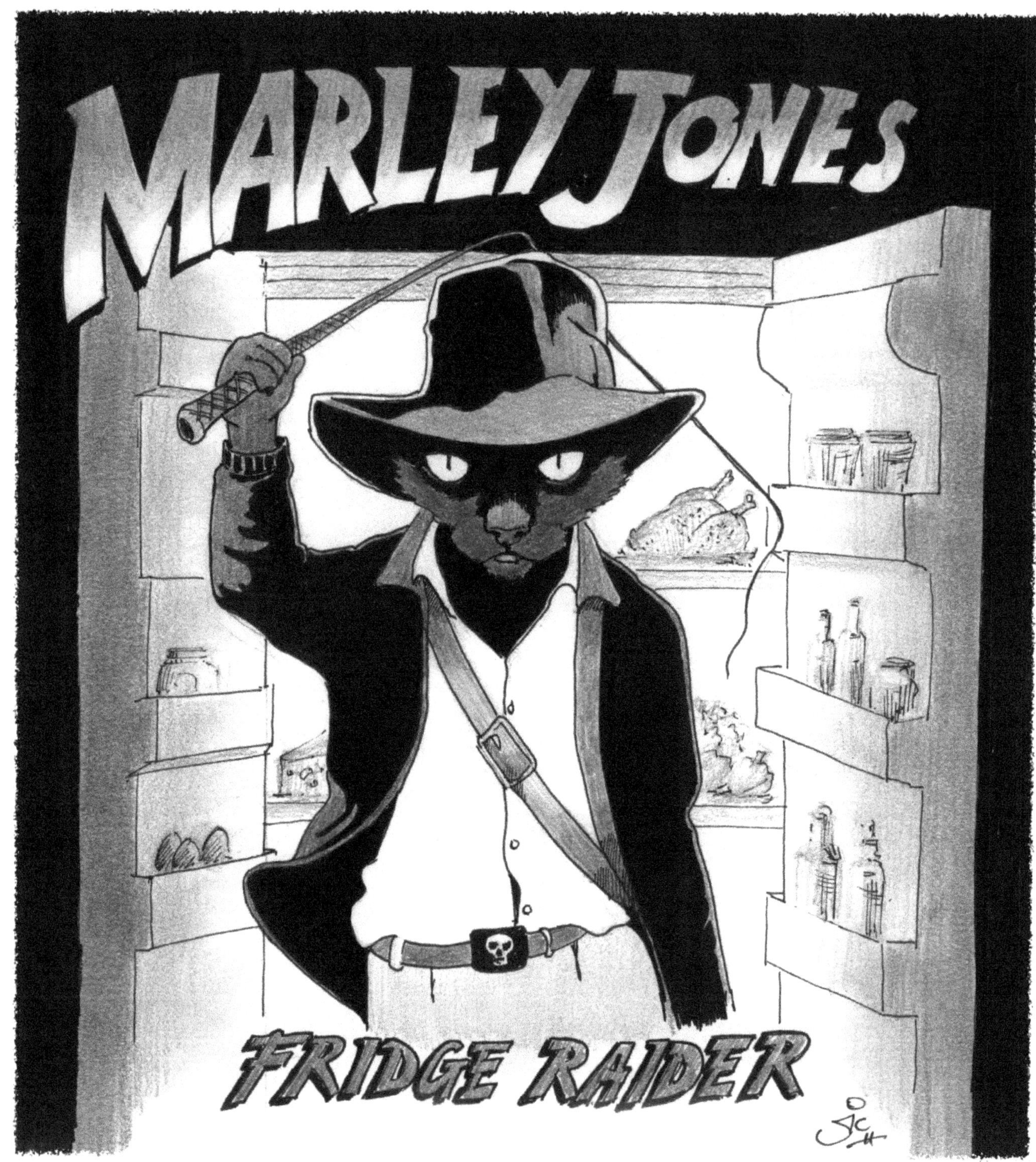

'Marley Jones'

Marley Stokes-Bearcroft is a mild-mannered professor of sleepology. His sensitive feline ears generally tuned out to most everyday comings and goings, save for one seemingly nondescript, quiet 'thwap' sound. At this, his ears prick up, eyes open with a wild stare, and his heavy-footed charge echoes through the house as he races, shrilling loudly, to the source of that sound... the fridge door! His aim is now a race against time to reach the fridge before the 'THWUMP' sound of the door closing.

Occasionally, he manages to reach high enough with his paw in a vain attempt to prevent the door closing, and, if he's quick enough, leaps into the brightly-lit vault to seek the treasure within... Elliott's chicken!

'Coming soon to a kitchen near you, 'Marley Jones and the Fridge of Doom.'

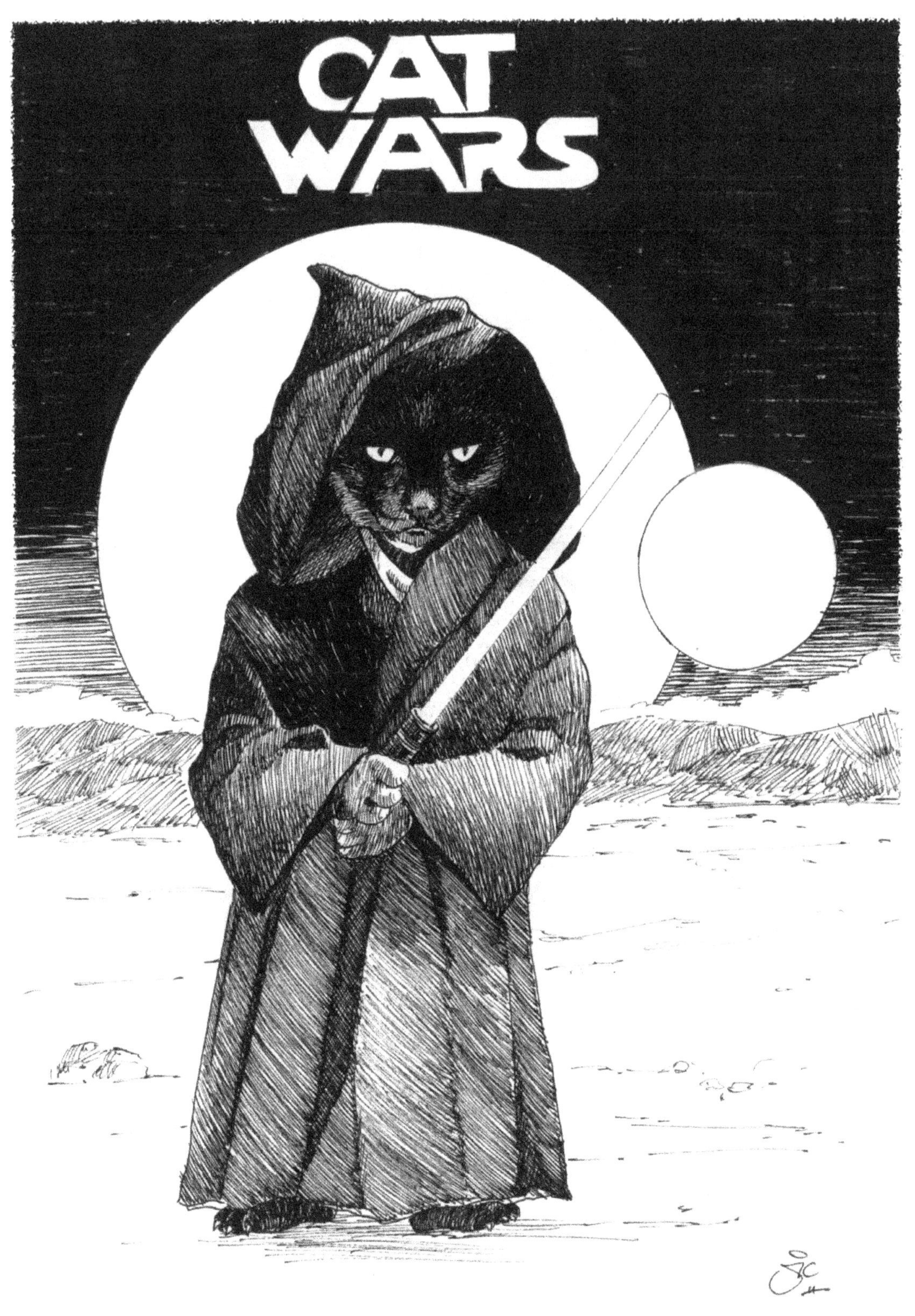

'Cat Wars'

Sometimes inspiration comes in the most unexpected forms. One evening I took a couple of phone shots of Marley peeking out from under a sofa throw. I thought he looked a bit like a monk perhaps. The following evening I settled down to watch the original Star Wars movie. Before too long, in my mind, I saw Marley as an Obi-wan Konobi character. Of course, then out came the sketchbook and pen. As often happens, I ended up not watching the movie at all!

Inspired by a re-reading of Treasure Island, Marley Fishbones is a character study for a future story, 'The Curse of the Black Feather'.

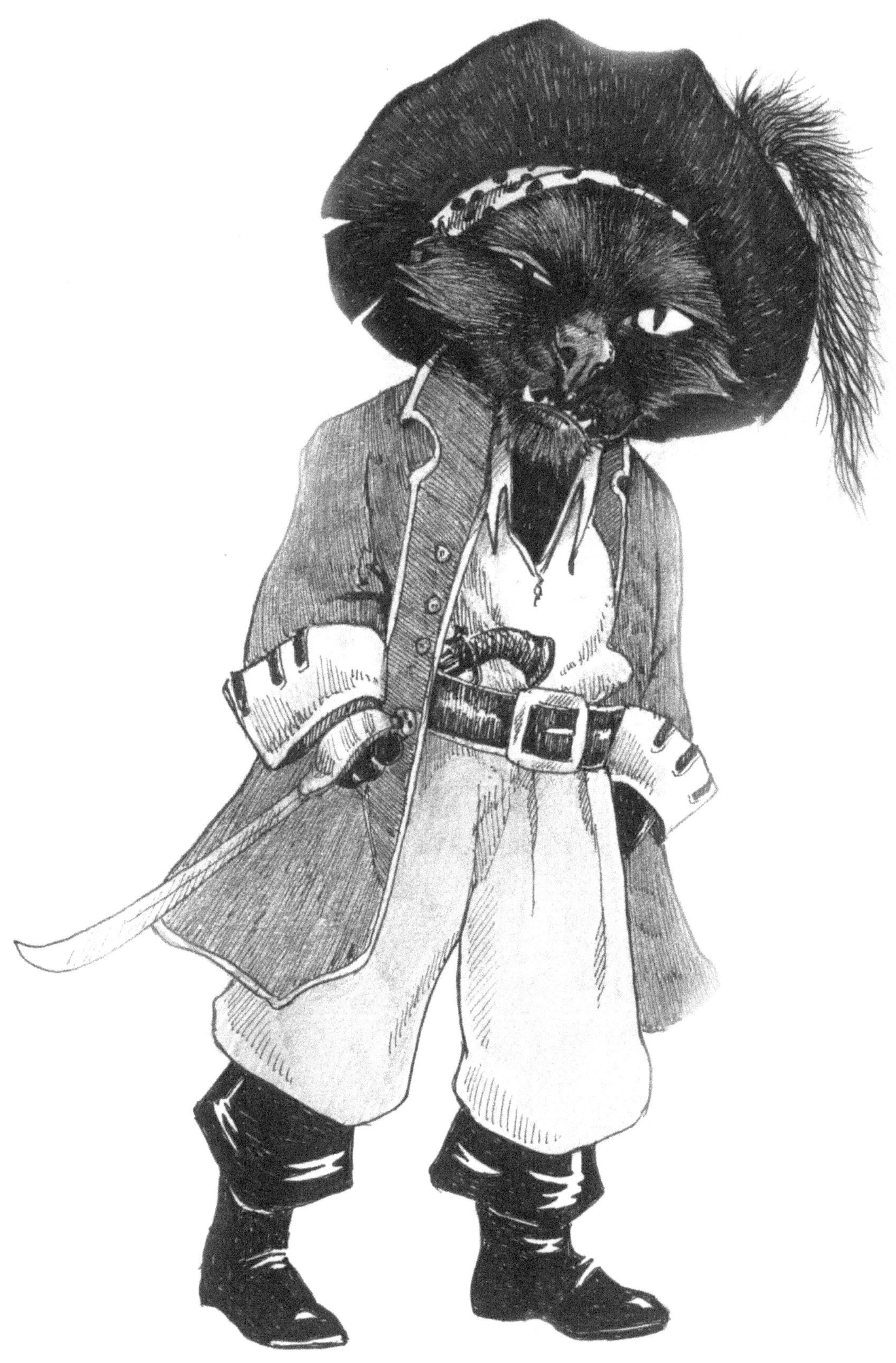

'Katnipped!

This is 'Captain Marley Fishbones' – 'On account of I likes fish so much, that there ain't nothin' left but bones when I've finished with 'em!'

Here are a couple more ink sketches inspired by our black cat Marley. Marley has a distinct vampire look, due to an injury he received as a kitten, before he adopted us. He's very sweet really, but he plays the 'evil' role quite convincingly.

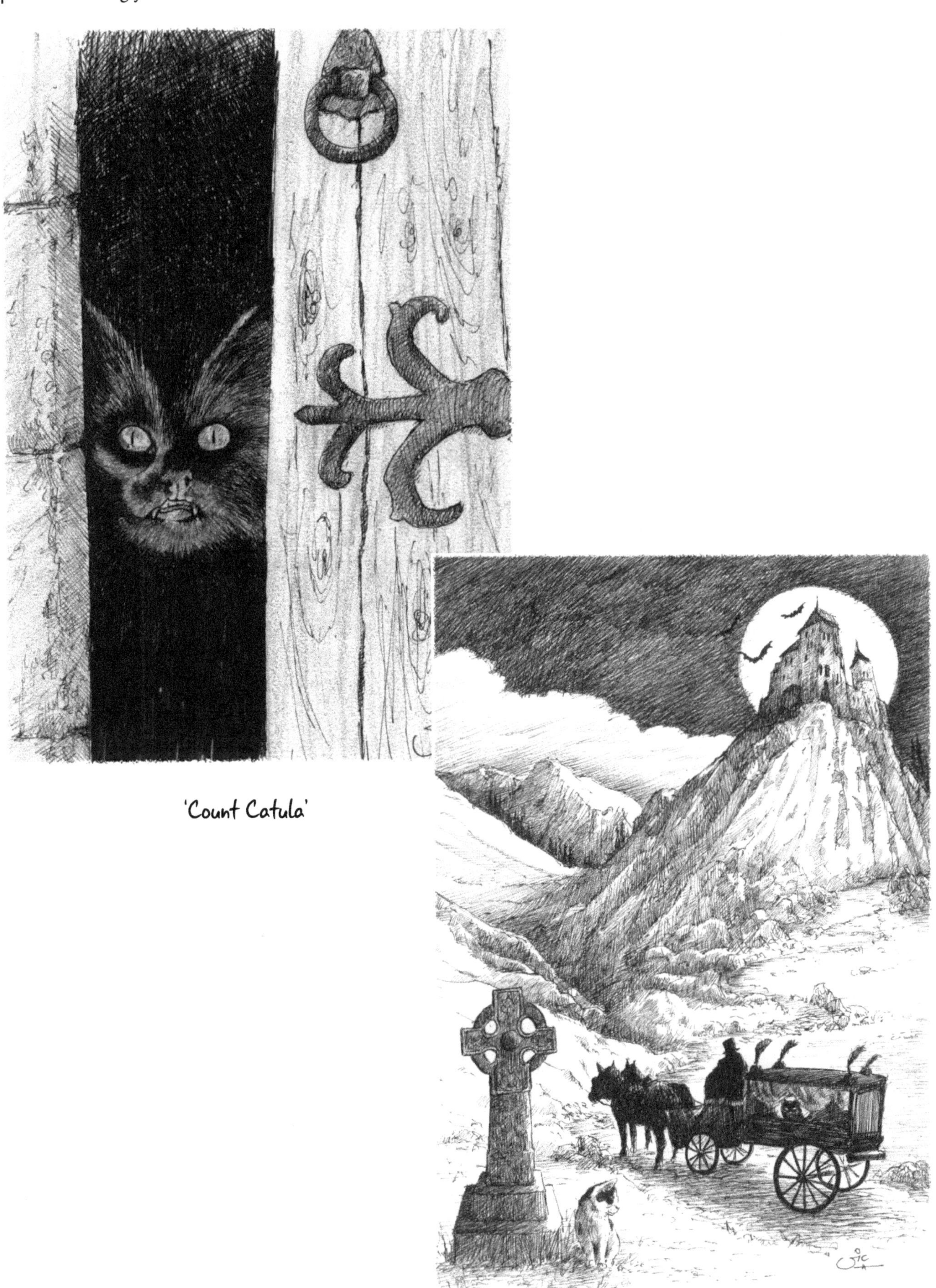

'Count Catula'

'Catula's Castle'

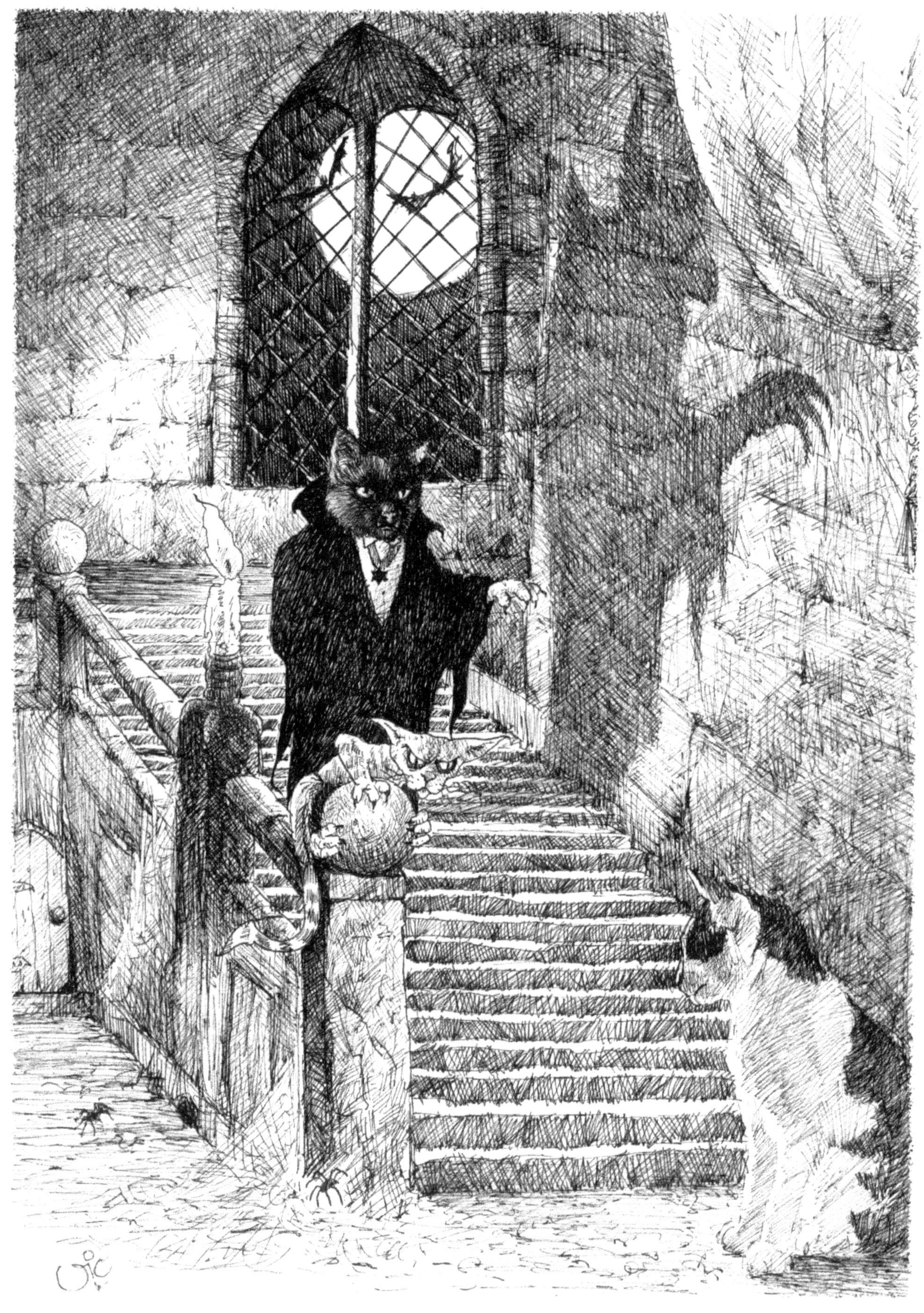

'The Kittens of the Night'

This is an extension, and, for now, the final instalment of the 'Count Catula' series. This sketch also features Oscar Wildecat as the Jonathan Harker character and Forrest, our only ginger cat, as a feline gargoyle.

Doodles

The following pages are dedicated to doodling.

Doodling is always fun, a five or ten minute distraction, or a constructive way to pass half an hour or so that can often be the spark which ignites creative ideas.

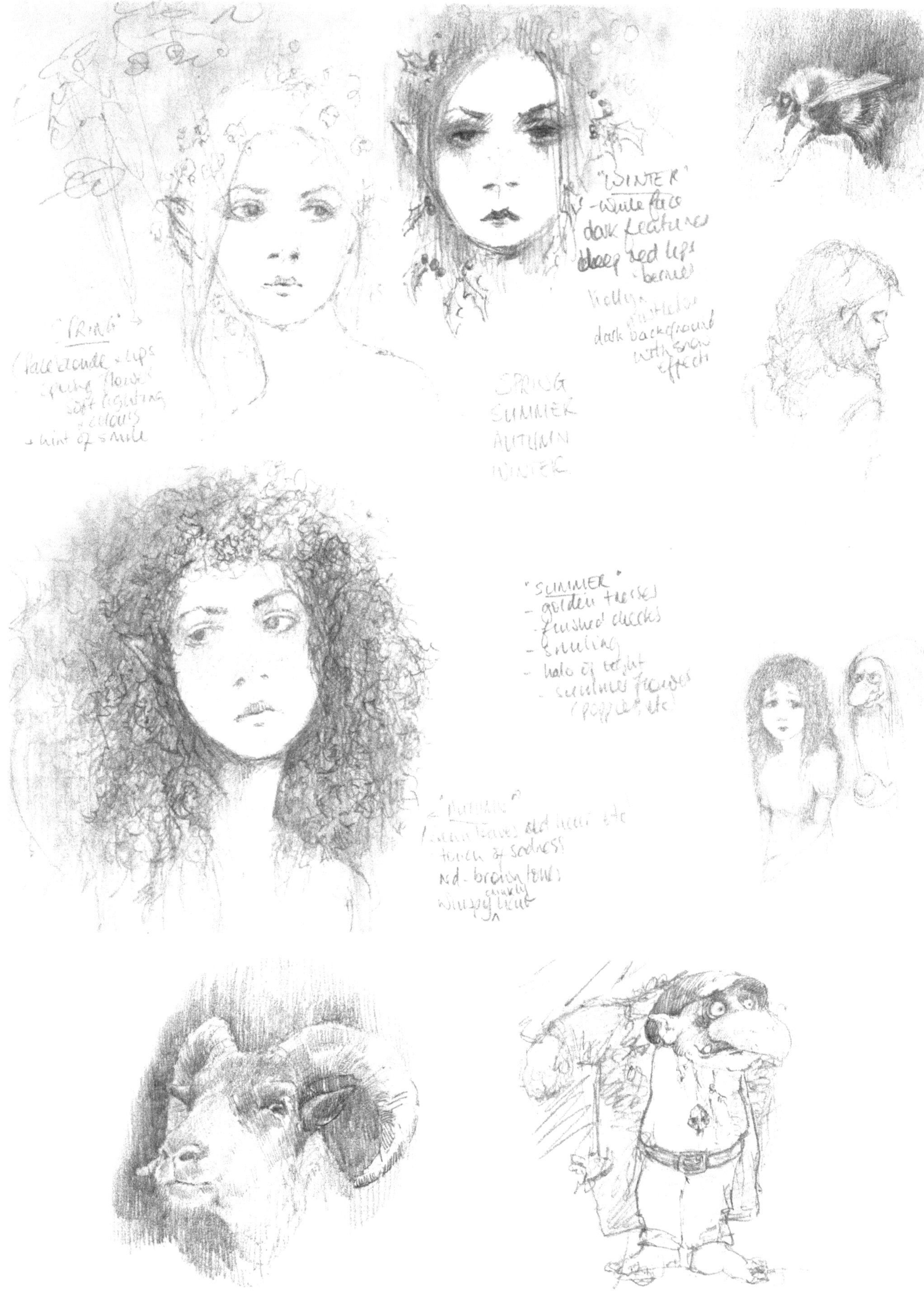

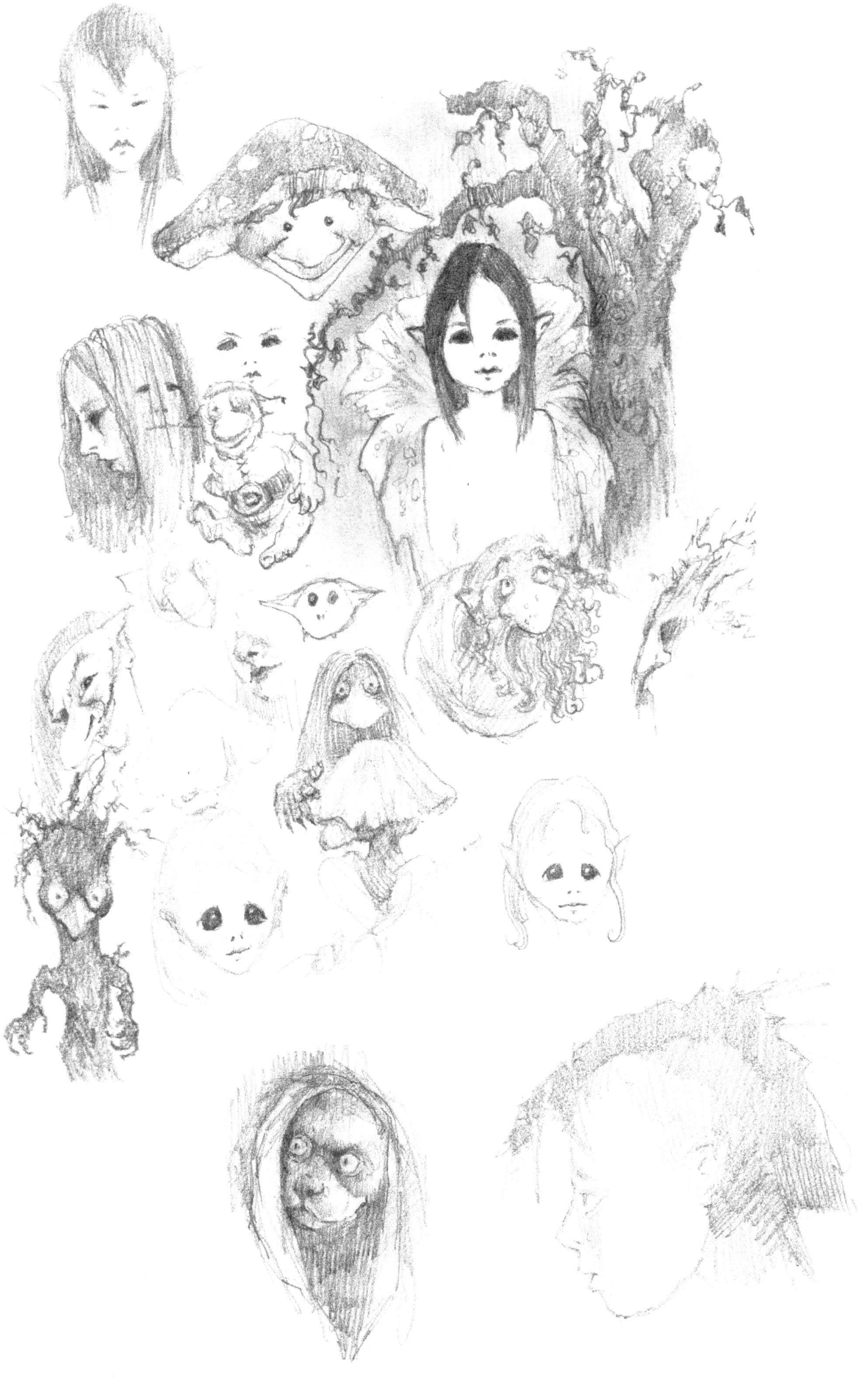

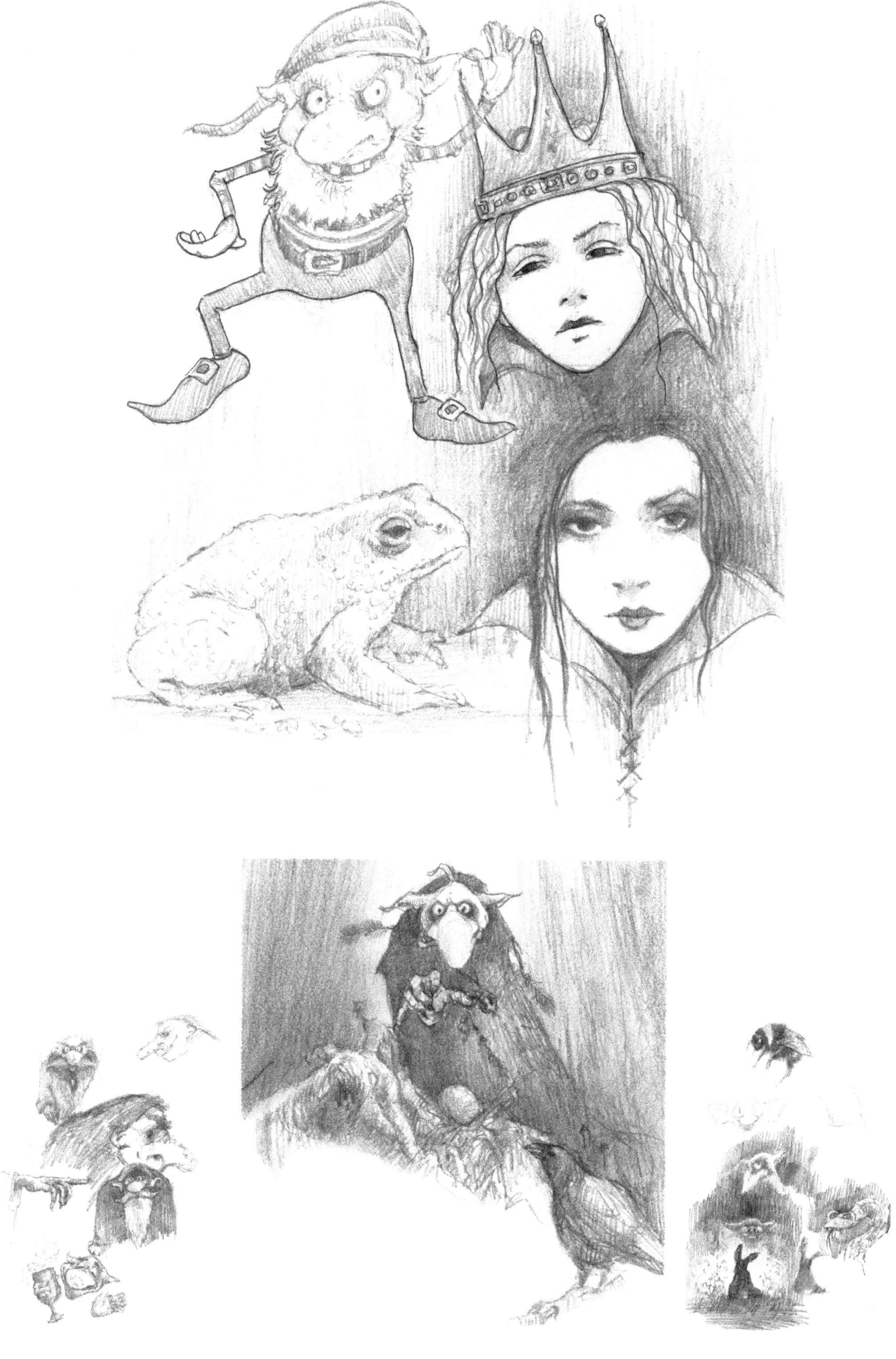

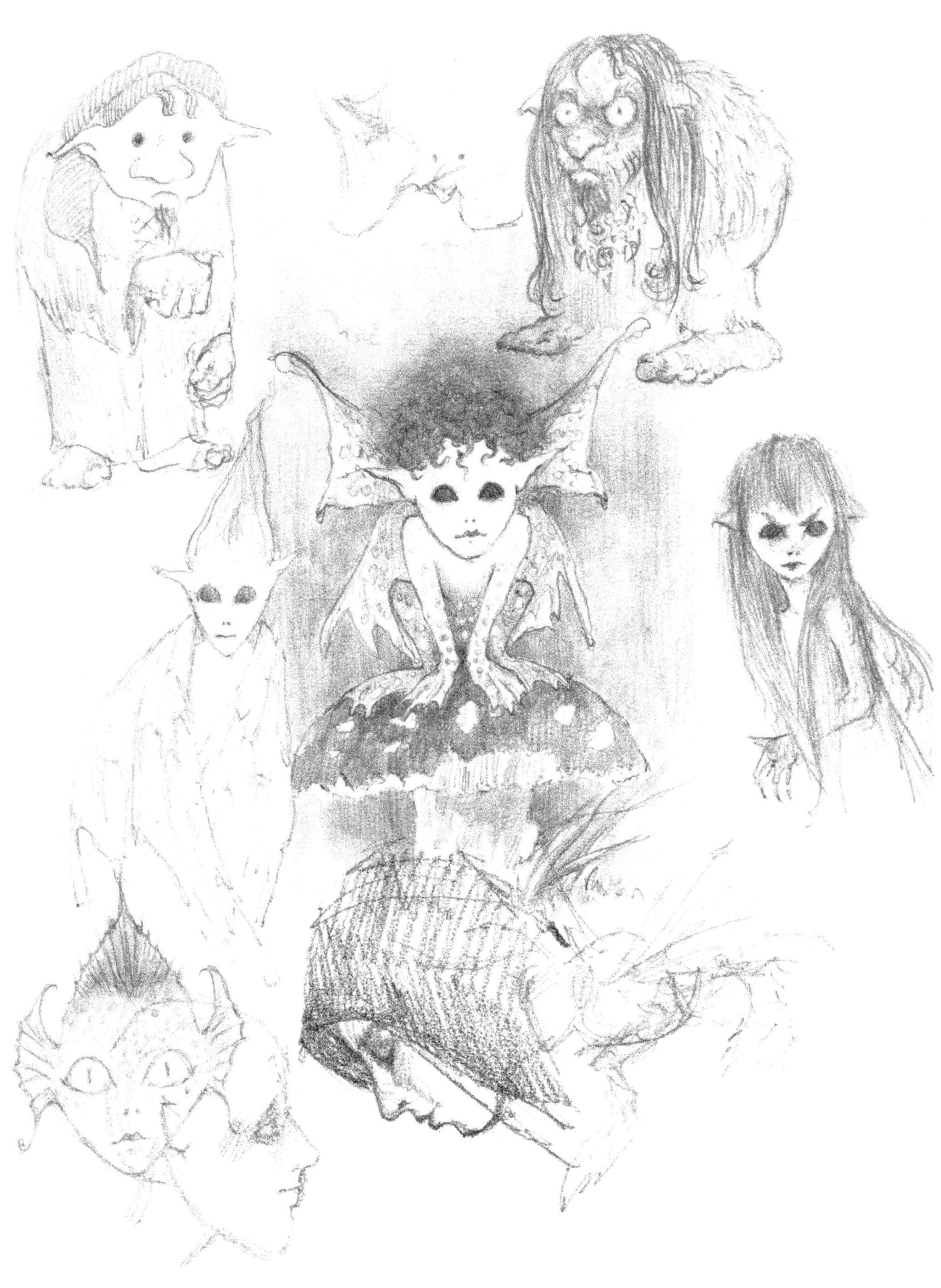

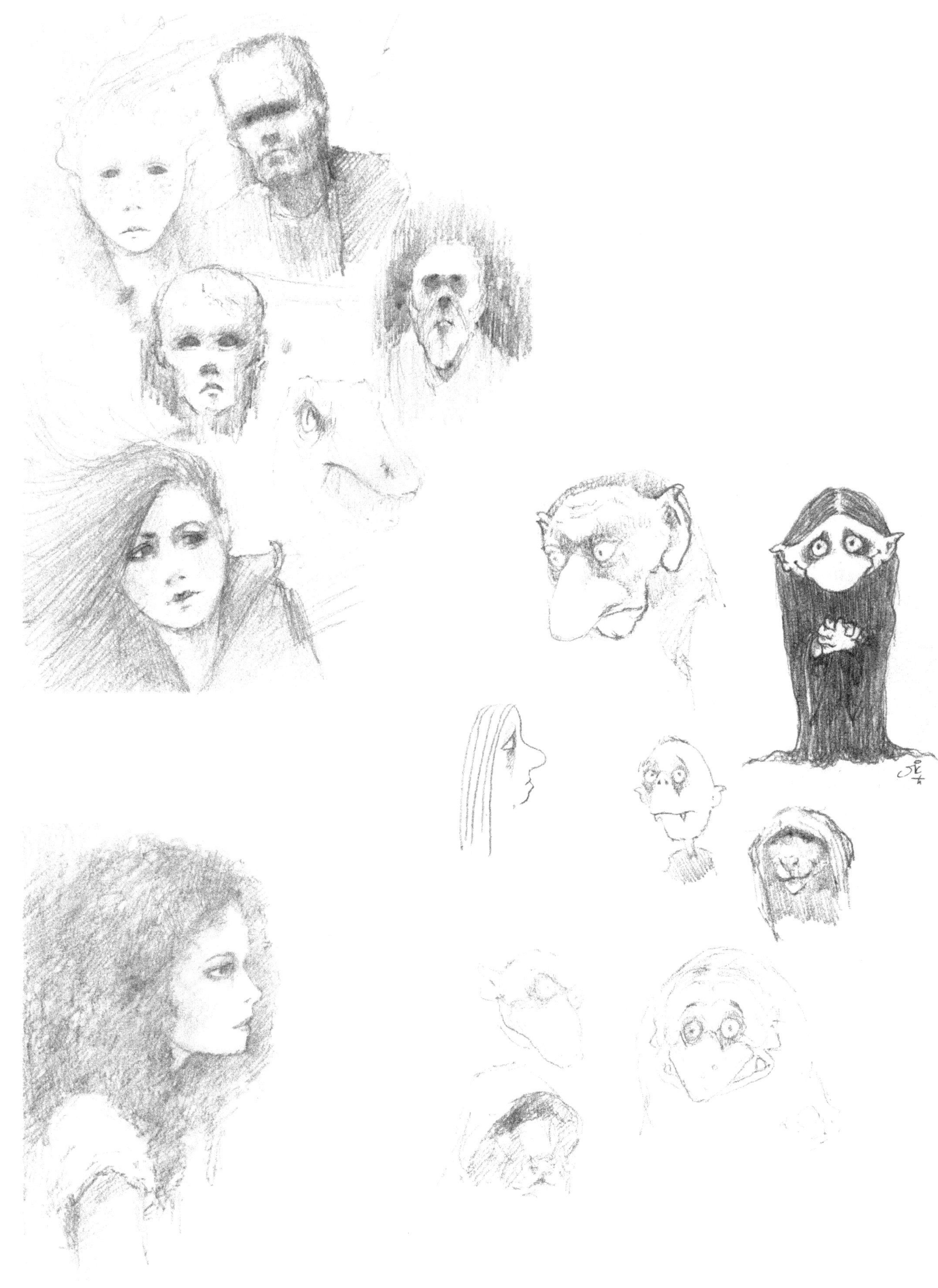

www.ingramcontent.com/pod-product-compliance
Ingram Content Group UK Ltd.
Pitfield, Milton Keynes, MK11 3LW, UK
UKHW060020300726
14090UKWH00020B/1082

9 780956 808035